THE
AMERICA'S
FINEST
COMPANIES
INVESTMENT
PLAN

THE
AMERICA'S
FINEST
COMPANIES
INVESTMENT
PLAN

Double Your Money
Every Five Years

Bill Staton

NEW YORK

Library of Congress Cataloging-in-Publication Data
Staton, Bill.

The America's finest companies investment plan : double your money every five years / by Bill Staton.
    p.   cm.
    ISBN 0-7868-8047-3
    1. Investments—United States.   2. Finance, Personal—United States.   I. Title.
    HG4910.S63   1994
    332.024′01—dc20   94-3055
                                                         CIP

FIRST EDITION
10 9 8 7 6 5 4 3 2 1

CONTENTS

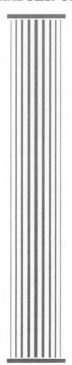

CHAPTER ONE

Why You Should Invest in America's Finest Companies

In the big book of things people more often do wrong than right, investing must certainly top the list, followed closely by wallpapering and eating artichokes.

—*THE MONEY BOOK OF MONEY*, 1987

Millions of Americans—you may be one of them—have all their hard-earned dollars locked away in banks because they think their money is "safe." But after taxes and inflation are taken out, they're behind the eight ball.

If most or all of your money is in savings accounts, certificates of deposit, and money-market funds, it's a scary time because interest rates are so low. You'd like an alternative way to put your money to work, but you're concerned about high fees and bum advice. You may have heard stocks are the way to go, but you know little if anything about them. You may have been burned by a broker who cared more about his commission than your money.

That's why I've developed an investment program you can use without relying on stockbrokers or other financial advisors. Making your money work for you ought to be fun and easy, safe and sure. You don't have to be a professional or spend every waking moment to build funds for your future. You don't have to take a lot of time from your own career and personal life. And you don't have to hand your money over to one of the more than 5,000 mutual funds.

Investing isn't voodoo or hocus-pocus. The word *invest* comes from the Latin *investire*—to commit for a long period with the thought of future benefit. To invest means to put money to work today so that it will earn more money for the future. You invest your money in something to reap a profit.

Investing (as opposed to speculating and taking unnecessary risks) is a process. A process is a series of actions leading to an end. By definition, then, investing is something you should start now, or should have already started, and plan to continue indefinitely. Stocks are the best—and the easiest—asset to invest in.

During my twenty-four years as a money coach, I've learned that individuals can get the most from their money just by following a few simple guidelines. My investment program is built around America's Finest Companies, and will show you how to be your own money manager. There is no Wall Street jargon, there are no complicated rules, no complex formulas, nothing to buy. Everything you need is within these pages.

I'll explain in plain English how the stock market works—why certain principles apply and a lot of others don't. I'll show you that stocks have provided a higher return than any other investment, including real estate, for more than a hundred years. You'll learn what it takes for a company to be one of America's Finest and why these companies have far outdistanced the stock market. You'll also learn the simple process of investing for maximum profits with least risk and how to develop your own list of America's Finest Companies to invest in.

My list of America's Finest Companies is compiled once each year and is eagerly awaited by my newsletter subscribers and the financial media. That's because these companies are the elite of corporate America—the top 3 percent of all public companies—with at least ten straight years of higher earnings or dividends per share.

Even if you think a company has to be one of America's Finest, you need to make sure. That's why this book is necessary. No company is included if it doesn't have at least ten straight years of higher earnings or dividends. America's Finest Companies are the thoroughbreds of corporate America.

You wouldn't go to the racetrack and bet on the nags, would you? That would be a sure way to lose money. Doesn't it make sense, then, that your hard-earned dollars, the dollars you're accumulating for your children's college education, a larger home, another car, retirement, or whatever, should be invested in shares of the finest companies you can buy? If you wouldn't bet your money on nags at the racetrack, you shouldn't bet your money on companies that aren't proven winners.

Building and managing your own "mini-mutual fund" of America's Finest will take very little time—one or two hours per year—and allow you to outperform 75 percent of the pros 100 percent of the time. Creating your own mini-mutual fund of America's Finest Companies is the best way I know to reach your financial goals. It's even better than investing in mutual funds. Why? Because America's Finest Companies deliver spectacular returns.

The 417 companies on the AFC list gained 93 percent in price for the five years ending December 31, 1993, compared with 68 percent for the popular Standard & Poor's 500 index. For the past ten years, AFC companies returned 328 percent compared with S & P's 183 percent. That's from price appreciation alone. With dividends included, the record is even better.

An ad in *The Wall Street Journal* led with this headline, "It's no surprise that the #1-ranked mutual fund for the last ten-year period is offered by Merrill Lynch." According to the ad, the total return on investment for the ten years ending June 30, 1993, for the Merrill Lynch Pacific Fund was 546.35 percent.

That's a phenomenal return, but doesn't approach the record achieved by the America's Finest Companies universe. Two hundred forty-seven of the companies had dividend reinvestment plans (I explain what these are and their awesome power in Chapter 8) in place at the end of 1982. For the ten years and three months between December 31, 1982, and March 31, 1993, the total return on investment was 739.5 percent, nearly 200 percent more than was generated by the top mutual fund over an almost identical period. One thousand dollars in America's Finest Companies grew to $8,740 compared to $6,464 in the Merrill Lynch fund.

This is an easy-to-read-and-understand guide to making money with the cream of American companies. I believe anyone can dramatically improve his or her financial health with my time-proven, powerful method, which is deceptively simple to implement. There are no gimmicks or tricks. A young person can begin to invest with as little as $500 and easily become a millionaire (even a multimillionaire) by retirement.

Since World War II, a diversified portfolio (group) of stocks has grown at 12 percent compounded annually, a higher return than from any other investment. Just by earning 12 percent each year, you'll regularly outperform 75 percent or more of all professional money managers. But you should be able to earn more than that—13–15 percent annually—with a diverse portfolio of America's Finest Companies. That doesn't sound much better than 12 percent, but, assuming you invest as little as $2,000 per year for thirty years, the 1–3 percent difference will be worth an additional $120,000 to $460,000.

One cardinal principle holds true: By buying only the shares of high-quality companies, you'll become a successful investor. You'll be part owner of companies that are in sound financial condition, that won't go out of business, and whose earnings and dividends will continue to grow.

A company must earn money to remain in business. Otherwise it will eventually go bankrupt. Part of those earnings are paid to investors in the form of cash dividends. The rest is plowed back for research and development; to bring new products or services to market; to buy new, more productive equipment; to hire more employees. All earnings put back into the company enhance the value of the business. As the value of the business rises, so does the price of the company's stock. It has to.

One excellent example of a company that's done a superior job enhancing the value of its business—and its share price—is Wal-Mart Stores, one of the brightest lights in America's Finest Companies. Wal-Mart is among a handful of companies with more than thirty consecutive years of higher earnings per share. Through the end of 1993, Wal-Mart had thirty-two straight years of rising earnings and ten of higher cash dividends paid out to owners of its stock. Since 1983 revenue skyrocketed from just under $5 billion to $67 billion ten years later. The share price exploded elevenfold, from under $3 to a shade over $30.

Wal-Mart and its founder, the late Sam Walton, are practically household words, as are a lot of America's Finest Companies—Coca-Cola, Clorox, DuPont, Exxon, Johnson & Johnson, Kmart, Merck, and Sara Lee to name a few. But there are just as many that are totally unfamiliar to most people, whether they are investors or not. For example, there's The Washington Real Estate Investment Trust. Ever heard of it? I hadn't either until three years ago.

Washington REIT—you guessed it—invests in real estate. It prides itself on being maverick, unorthodox, and conservative. The company mails some of the most interesting annual and quarterly reports to shareholders. These reports tell how the company is doing. A 1993 quarterly noted the company moved out of its old headquarters (after selling it for a tenfold profit) into the basement of its new WRIT Building. I've never before seen a company press release about abandoning offices with windows for offices without. But Washington REIT isn't your typical enterprise. In early 1993 the company burned its last outstanding mortgage in the company stove and toasted a few marshmallows in the process. To be on the safe side, they asked the building fire marshall to stand by with a fire extinguisher, and they also mailed a press release about this extraordinary event.

Washington REIT does more than mail witty notices to the press and its shareholders. It earns lots of money. By the end of 1993, the company had put together a total of fifty years of higher earnings and dividends per share, a record fewer than twenty other public companies (out of more than fifteen thousand) can match. For the past twenty years, the stock returned 16 percent annually, triple the rate of inflation, compared to about 12 percent for stocks on the whole. One thousand dollars invested at the end of 1972 is worth more than $20,000 today. Over the past fifteen years the stock grew at 18 percent, and at 19 percent in the last ten-, five-, and one-year periods. Again, that's a record few other companies or professional money managers can match.

If you want to begin your own investment program, you can quickly name ten or twelve financially sound companies whose earnings or dividends will continue to grow well into the future. How do I know that? Because everywhere I have led a workshop on investing, I've asked the audience to choose a portfolio of five to eight companies. In every instance to date, they've picked high-quality companies in a variety of industries. The majority of the companies they pick are in my universe of America's Finest. That is, they have at least ten years in a row of increasing earnings or dividends per share, establishing them as the top 3 percent of all public companies.

Of course, you may be thinking, "Why should I be in stocks at all? They're too risky. Look how far they fell during the Crash of 1987—23 percent in one day. That was worse than in the Great Depression. I wouldn't own any stocks. I couldn't sleep at night if I did."

If you're thinking that, you're not alone. The most frequent comments I hear about stocks and the stock market are negative. (I use the term *market, stock market,* and *market indexes* interchangeably. They mean the same thing in the investment world.) Here are a few I've heard in my seminars:

"High risk/high reward." (the emphasis is always on high risk).

"Frothy." (picture a rabid dog foaming at the mouth).

"A bottomless pit."

"Extremely volatile."

"Too complicated."

"A loser's game."

"Only an expert should try it."

"Like walking down a dark alley in a crime-infested neighborhood."

"I'd rather visit the dentist."

I do hear positives, too, but they're normally about as few as friends in a cobra pit. It's been like this for the twenty-four years I've been in the investment field.

Let's suppose you'd been in my office in December 1979 asking me what you should do with your money in the eighties and nineties. I would have said, "You should invest all the money you can in stocks, but first there are a few things you ought to know.

"An actor will become President of the United States and will preside over the biggest budget deficits in the nation's history. The deepest recession since the 1930s will occur in 1981–82. Nearly 20 percent of the workforce will be unemployed at some point during that period. There'll be another recession in 1990–91, in which that high percentage will again be without jobs.

"The biggest crash in stock-market history will occur in fall 1987, followed by a 'crashette' of huge proportions two years later. And oh, by the way, there'll be war in the Middle East with the United States leading the charge. A new plague—AIDS—will crop up around the world, plus there'll be record droughts and floods and some record-shattering hurricanes, too. There will also be a collapse of the dollar, scattered depressions in various states, a record number of personal, bank, and S&L bankruptcies, alongside numerous criminal convictions on Wall Street.

"Crime will appear virtually out of control in many major cities, and a riot in Los Angeles will turn out to be the most expensive in history. Some of the largest corporations in America will lay off employees ten thousand at a time.

"Now, do you still want to buy some stocks?" Your answer, most likely, would have been a resounding "No." Yet that would have been a bad answer. Between 1980 and today, stocks outperformed bonds, stamps, Treasury bills (roughly the equivalent of a savings account), diamonds, oil, gold, housing, the cost of living, Chinese ceramics, farmland, foreign currency, and silver. Stocks as a class were by far the number-one investment. Shares of America's Finest Companies were even better. There was no close second.

If you picture investing in stocks as buying pieces of paper that go up and down in value every day like yo-yos, I understand why you might be hesitant about owning shares of any companies, whether they're America's Finest or not. But you don't have to look at them that way. A better viewpoint is that you become part owner of one or more of the finest businesses in this country.

My guess is that if you had enough money, you wouldn't mind owning all of Coca-Cola or Wal-Mart or Exxon or Tootsie Roll Industries or Colgate-Palmolive or Procter & Gamble or McDonald's or many others in the America's Finest universe. You know they're well-established corporations with superior credentials. You also know that year after year their earnings and dividends will continue to grow, and you have no reason to suspect they won't remain viable for as long as you live and even for decades after that.

At this point, you might respond, "But what about companies like General Motors and IBM? They used to be among the best companies in America, but then had so much difficulty in recent years. Their stocks collapsed. I don't want to go through the agony of seeing one of my stocks fall from 176 to a low of 41 the way IBM did."

My answer is "I'll show you a foolproof technique in Chapter 7 that will allow you to make substantial profits in any environment—including the Great Depression—as long as you invest in companies that don't go out of business. Both GM and IBM, even though their share prices gave up a lot of ground, are still in business, so you could eventually make money if you own them. But neither is among America's Finest Companies because they don't meet my strict requirement of subsequently higher annual earnings or dividends."

Even though you don't have the billions of dollars it would take to buy a Wal-Mart or PepsiCo and make it your own, you do have enough money to buy a few shares of one, if not both, of these companies. Those shares or pieces of the business represent your proportionate ownership of Coca-Cola, McDonald's, or whatever else you buy. They're great businesses to own parts of, and they're bound to increase in value over the long term—the next five, ten, fifteen, twenty years, or more—because the values of their businesses are growing every year. That hasn't been the case with GM and IBM.

By assembling a portfolio of at least five of America's Finest Companies, each in a different industry, and adding to the portfolio on a regular basis (preferably annually), you should regularly double your money every five to six years. That's far faster than from any other investment.

By investing only in corporate thoroughbreds, you can take a lot of worry from your shoulders. You can quit worrying about inflation, interest rates, government legislation, recessions, etc., and how they will affect your investments. Since you're only going to invest in the best American industry has to offer, you can let the companies do the worrying for you.

Think of yourself barreling down a river of white water like the Gauley in West Virginia, which has the fiercest rapids east of the Mississippi. I've rafted the entire length of this beautiful river three times. You have to cross the world's largest earthen dam to get to the foot of the Gauley. It's extremely intimidating to look well over a hundred feet down at the treacherous water gushing through the chutes at the bottom of the dam. The roar of the water pushing through is so loud it's hard to hear anyone talk.

I was mildly terrified (all right, I was scared to death) the first time we put our raft into the water, despite the fact I knew we had a reliable guide to get us safely through the roughest parts. Contrary to what I thought, the most dangerous part of white-water rafting isn't shuttling through the turbulent rapids. It's other people clowning around with the paddles and hitting one another in the face. The next most dangerous thing is trying to stand up in the fast-moving shallow water and getting a foot caught under a rock. That's an easy way to drown.

The Gauley River isn't menacing when you know what you're doing. Buying shares of America's Finest Companies isn't menacing either because these companies know what they're doing and have proven it over the past ten years or longer. They know how to circumnavigate problems in business and the economy and take maximum advantage of the opportunities. That's why they're America's Finest. Placing your money on a portfolio of them is as sure a bet as you can make. Nearly two hundred years of American investment history proves that.

As "America's Money Coach," I don't tell Americans what they should do with their money, nor do I do it for them. By definition, I am a trainer, an instructor, an investment guide. I am not a drill sergeant. I coach people to manage their money themselves, to take charge of their financial affairs and to achieve financial security. I learned what I know the hard way.

Having graduated from an Ivy League school with an MBA in 1971, I toured Europe for twelve weeks with my roommate and then settled down as a freshman analyst with Interstate Securities (now Interstate/Johnson Lane) in Charlotte, North Carolina. Interstate had a small equity (stock) research department with a CPA, a nice fellow, as its director. One of the early lessons I learned at Interstate was never to make a CPA head of your research department. They may know their numbers, but they're usually not the greatest stock pickers.

Since I knew virtually nothing about stocks, the stock market, investing, or the economy, I was immediately assigned to review customer portfolios and make suggestions about what to buy and to sell. I'm glad our customers didn't know how little I knew. At the time, even I didn't realize how little I knew, but somehow I muddled through.

Three years into my career, the stock market entered a protracted bear market (bear markets fall, bull markets rise) that wouldn't finish killing investors until December 1974, two years after it began. This bear market was the most savage since the 1930s. It was my first but certainly not my last. The closing Dow Jones industrial average (the principal market index), which Dan Rather now reports every night on CBS, peaked in early 1973 at 1052 and finally troughed about twenty-four months later at 578, a 45 percent plunge.

Most of the stocks I and my department of analysts were recommending did far worse. Some fell 80 percent or more, and that was not particularly atypical. Brokerage houses across America were enduring similar fates. Besides all my recommendations being pounded beneath the floor, I lost about 75 percent of my personal portfolio in the carnage. After it was all over but while I was still thinking the world might end any day, I decided it was time to take a different tack. By then I had been put in charge of the research efforts. Toward the end of 1975 I was officially named research director and an officer of the firm.

By this point, three important lessons were engraved in my cranium:

1. Don't let a CPA run your research department.
2. Make sure an analyst knows what he's doing before you turn him loose on your customers.
3. Bear markets hurt.

Armed with these invaluable bits of wisdom, I set out on a quest to discover (1) how to keep from losing money, and (2) how to make substantial profits investing in companies. I had just entered a three-year program to become a chartered financial analyst (CFA), which is the security-analyst equivalent of a CPA in accounting. The most important thing I learned in the CFA program was discovering a book called *Security Analysis* by Benjamin Graham and David Dodd. Though this book was no longer used in the program, I found out it was a book I needed to own, so I purchased it and began the slow slog through its six-hundred-plus pages.

I uncovered one concept Graham developed—margin

of safety—and took it to heart. There's more about this in Chapter 3, Valuable Lessons from Benjamin Graham. Warren Buffett, Graham's best and wealthiest student (he's worth more than $8 billion) at Columbia, likened margin of safety to building a bridge to accommodate forty tons, but nothing heavier than ten tons ever crosses it.

As Interstate's research director, I urged all the analysts to become students of Benjamin Graham and to adhere strictly to the margin-of-safety concept. In late 1974, contrary to the industry, we began keeping records of all our recommendations and how they stacked up against the market indexes. We also told our brokers and customers that when we thought it was time to sell a stock we'd say so in writing. Margin of safety worked. The research record, published annually, served as a check. When I left Interstate at the end of 1985, our research department had compiled an eleven-year performance record that was the envy of Wall Street.

Since I began my newsletter, *Bill Staton's Money Advisory,* in January 1986, I have published my record frequently. Every stock recommended to my clients (from the time I say buy to when I say sell) gained an average 30.7 percent annualized, compared with 11.8 percent for Standard & Poor's 500 index. That's a record few other money experts can touch.

Now that I've shown you my track record, you're going to learn why stocks have always been, and will continue to be, the most profitable investment. The historical evidence is overwhelming, so I'll show you only a little of it. From there, you'll learn the value of a simple investment program. We'll examine what it takes for a company to become one of America's Finest, and you'll get an up-close look at 4 of the 417 that constitute the AFC universe.

Although it's tempting to pay a professional to take charge of your money, in most cases I don't recommend it. You really can have superior results if you do it yourself. My daughter, who's sixteen now, started her own portfolio at age ten, using my America's Finest Companies criteria, and since then has beat two-thirds of the pros, doubling the return of the market indexes. Since May 1988 through January 31, 1994, the initial $4,300 investment has swelled to more than $10,600. If she can do it, why can't you?

Good old Uncle Sam and the state where you live will gladly help you make more money if you'd be interested in deferring taxes for years, if not decades, down the road. Most people don't know how to take advantage of Uncle's generosity, but I'll teach you how to make it work for you.

Being your own money manager sounds like a lot of hard work, but really it isn't. Is sixty minutes too much time to spend each year? That's the time most Americans use for lunch each day. I'm only asking for about one hour annually. That's all it takes, and you can become a million-aire if you'll stick with this easy-to-start-and-maintain investment program. If you don't need the annual cash dividends from your stocks for personal use, I'll show you how to make them make more money. I'll even show you how to buy shares direct and bypass the stockbroker. You can save thousands of dollars over a lifetime of investing.

You have to open your investment account somewhere. The mechanics aren't difficult. I'll show you how to get started the easiest way.

Do you want to embark your children on an investment program as I did with my daughter in 1988? The earlier they start, the more successful they'll be. What about giving money and securities to your children? We'll look at that option, too. Then we'll move into the companies themselves. There are 417 listed in the Appendix at the back of the book along with lots of helpful statistics. There's plenty of good merchandise from which to choose. There's something for everybody.

CHAPTER TWO

Stocks Are the Number-One Investment

It makes me nervous when I'm not nervous about the stock market.

—WILLIE WONDER

Millions of Americans are afraid to buy shares of companies. They get goose bumps just thinking about putting money into stocks, even of the top-rated companies, because they reason that one day prices might go over the cliff as they did between 1929 and 1932. Investing in stocks is as terrifying to them as skydiving would be to me. That's why I don't do it—skydiving that is.

Besides this large group that doesn't want to enter investment waters with stocks as the vehicle, there's a second large group—those who own shares of companies but are antsy during the day and don't sleep well at night either. They're like my fictitious friend Willie Wonder. They're always nervous about stocks. When stocks go down, they worry they'll fall further. When stocks go up, they worry they'll soon stop going up and then go down. Or if they don't know which way stock prices are headed, they worry that they don't know and that the direction might not be the way they want to go. These people are worrywarts and don't need to be. They're like the person George Burns described "who feels bad when he feels good for fear that he'll feel worse when he feels better."

If you fit into either of these categories, I want to convince you: Stocks are a great place to have your money, the safest, least risky place of all. Just for the moment, put aside any hesitation you may have and accept these words. You can always change your mind later. I believe that when you finish this chapter you'll know why stocks have always been, and will continue to be, the number-one investment. I don't want you to feel about investing in stocks as Gertrude Stein, the American writer, did about life in general, "There ain't any answer. There ain't going to be any answer. There never has been an answer. That's the answer."

Before we get into why stocks are right for almost everyone, I'll share a little history about how stocks came to be and why they *always* go up when given enough time.

By the time Columbus set sail for what he thought were the East Indies (he landed in the Caribbean instead), shares of various commodities and what were then called joint-stock companies were actively bought and sold in Antwerp, Belgium. The city of Antwerp claims that, of the world's 140-odd stock exchanges, its exchange is the oldest, having been founded in 1531. Amsterdam lays claim to the second with a start-up date of 1602.

Stock certificates of ownership were sold to investors in some European countries to finance powerhouse enterprises like the United East India Company, which came to life in 1602. This phenomenal company returned about 18 percent annually to investors for three decades ($1 grew to more than $143), an incredible performance, and remained in business until 1799.

Stock trading on a limited basis existed well before Jesus was born. The early Romans formed joint-stock companies and sold pieces of them to the public. The word *company* is from *cum* (with) and *panis* (bread) because business, even in those days, was often conducted over a meal, as it so frequently is today. Under the law, joint-stock companies of that time could do just two things— government contracting and tax collecting. What fantastic businesses to invest in! Capital (money) was raised by selling *partes* (shares) to willing investors.

Securities markets in the United States can be traced to the late 1700s. In 1789, Congress authorized and issued $80 million of government bonds to pay down war debts and to inject money into this fledgling country's economy, thereby creating the first "money market." According to *American Heritage* magazine, "The new United States was desperately short of money in any reliable or secured form. Accounts were still kept in pounds, shillings, and pence."

Brokers (they were first called stockjobbers) traded securities literally in the street. The word *broker* was derived from wine merchants, who broached (tapped) their wine kegs. *Broacher* was later shortened to *broker*. Brokers bought and sold primarily government bonds as well as any stocks offered by the infant Bank of the United States. When the weather turned sour, they retreated to coffeehouses (presumably to warm up) and carried on their business.

The several dozen established brokers operated a highly risky "market." James Madison was so concerned he fired off a letter to Thomas Jefferson warning that "stock jobbing drowns every other subject. The coffeehouse is an eternal buzz with the gamblers." Since stock brokering, trading, or whatever you want to call it was so risky in the early days, the phrase "gambling in the stock market" still has deep meaning for most Americans.

In 1792, twenty-four brokers and merchants gathered at Corre's Hotel to sign the Buttonwood Agreement, which was written front and back on a sheet of paper:

> We, the Subscribers, Brokers for the Purchase and Sale of Public Stocks, do hereby solemnly pledge ourselves to each other that we will not buy or sell, from this day, for any person whatsoever, any kind of Public Stock at a less rate than one-quarter per cent Commission on the Special value, and that we will give preference to each other in our negotiations.

This unusual contract laid the foundation for the later-to-be-formed (in 1817) New York Stock & Exchange Board. The following winter the brokers built a home for themselves, the Tontine Coffee House, on the corner of Water and Wall streets in New York, then the nation's capital.

The famous street named Wall, one of the best known in the world, is only four blocks long. It lies on the site of the original wall (stockade) built at the tip of Manhattan Island. In 1644, Dutch settlers laid a brushwood barrier to keep Indians out and cattle in. Nine years later Governor Peter Stuyvesant replaced it with a nine-foot-high palisade. Wall Street is named for this barrier, not for the high buildings on both sides of the street that currently create walls.

"Wall Street" is the common name for the American financial institutions, markets, and mechanisms that formalized and democratized the capital-formation (money-raising) process that helps companies thrive. Wall Street, with the New York Stock Exchange as its flagship, has allowed millions of Americans to participate in this country's unmatched growth through ownership of common stocks. *Life* magazine, in its spring 1992 issue, dedicated to the Big Board, observed, "For two centuries, men (and, much more recently, women) have met at the convergence of Wall and Broad streets in lower Manhattan to buy, sell and haggle, all in the name of capitalism. They have not always done so politely . . . or fairly. But as Americans traded, so the country was built. Canals, Railroads, Automobiles, Electronics. Ideas may spring from laboratories, but the money that turns them into reality is raised here."

With capitalism rapidly spreading across the globe, new stock exchanges have recently sprouted behind what used to be the Iron Curtain. Poland opened a stock market in early 1991 in the old Communist Party headquarters (ironic, isn't it?). The Polish market was funded by British money and modeled after France's Bourse, another name for stock exchange or place of meeting to conduct business. Initially, trading took place only once a week in five different companies, but the government expects lots more, since it plans to privatize more than 3,500 firms under its control. Communist Party headquarters must be luxurious because St. Petersburg opened its exchange (*The Wall Street Journal* calls a stock exchange the "icon of capitalism") on the third floor of its own party building.

What exactly is a common stock? It's a security (stock certificate) representing proportionate ownership (an investor's share) of a publicly traded company. There are more than fifteen thousand public companies in America. You can buy shares in most of them through any stockbroker. These shares are traded (bought and sold) on either the New York Stock Exchange (NYSE), the American Stock Exchange (ASE), or Nasdaq Over-the-Counter (OTC). They range in price from a penny to more than $17,000 for Berkshire-Hathaway on the NYSE.

Where did the word *stock* come from? Here's my theory. William Bradford, governor of the Plymouth Colony, reported that under an agreement with the Pilgrims' sponsors from England, "all profit" (crops, fish, and trade goods) would "remain still in the common stock." All Pilgrims were allowed to obtain their food and goods from the common stock (to share), just as all investors can make their profits by investing (sharing) in the "common stock" of public companies.

Stocks are priced in points instead of dollars. One point equals $1.00. One-half point equals $0.50, one-quarter point $0.25, one-eighth point $0.125. Stocks trade in eighths rather than tenths like money. Isn't that strange? There's a practical reason. When stock trading began in colonial days, coins were in short supply. To make coinage go further, Spanish silver dollars were sliced into halves, then halved and halved again. The result? The dollar could be divided into eight bits. Each bit was one-eighth of a dollar. Together, eight bits became a "piece of eight."

Here's how stocks work. In this example, MakeMoney Enterprises (MME), a fictitious company, has one million shares outstanding. Each share sells for 20 (note: stock prices are quoted without the dollar sign), so MME's total stock is worth $20 million. If you invest $4,000 in MME at its current price, you can purchase two hundred shares.

When you purchase your shares, you will own part of the company. Although it's a tiny part (1/5000th), it's all yours. Now that you are part owner of MME, what good is it? Let's use this example to find out.

MME earns $2 million after taxes in 1995. Dividing earnings by the number of shares (1 million), each share has $2.00. MME provides money out of earnings, a cash dividend, as incentive for you to buy and hold its shares. (Not all companies pay dividends, but the bulk of America's Finest Companies do.) Out of the $2.00 per share of earnings, MME pays you half, $1.00. The dollar is your immediate reward for owning a piece of the company. MME keeps (retains) the other half and plows it back into the business for reasons similar to humans eating daily to survive. Retained earnings go for research and product development, to build a new plant, to purchase new equipment, to hire more people—to grow.

By keeping the dollar not paid you, MME is now worth

	1995	2000	2005
MME share price	20	??	??
MME earnings per share	$2.00	$3.00	$5.00
MME dividend per share	$1.00	$1.50	$2.50
MME keeps (retains)	$1.00	$1.50	$2.50

$1.00 more per share for each share outstanding than before. The company's total asset value increases $1 million (1 million shares times $1.00 per share retained). MME's business prospers. Five years from now its earnings have risen 50 percent to $3.00 per share. And as further reward to you for holding the shares as opposed to selling them, the company boosts its dividend (as it has done every year since you bought your shares) to the newest annual rate of $1.50. Each year it keeps as much as it pays you, and that amount kept annually enhances MME's value.

Your annual income is increasing. By 2005, earnings per share are $5.00. Your dividend is now $2.50 per share, up 150 percent over 1995. The company keeps $2.50 per share that year, $2.5 million total, to further boost asset value by that amount.

QUESTION: If the share price is 20 in 1995 when you buy into MME, and the shares are not overpriced, do you think the price will be higher in 2000 than in 1995? Will it be even higher in 2005?

ANSWER: If the share price maintains the same relationship to its earnings and dividend, it will rise to 30 in 2000 and to 50 by 2005.

Your original investment of two hundred shares at 20 each will be worth $10,000 in 2005. Your cost: $4,000. Your profit: $6,000. Between 1995 and 2005, your annual income from MME will jump from $200 to $500. Your yield on original investment will rise to 12.5 percent ($500 divided by $4,000), a handsome return.

Over a period of years, the majority of publicly owned companies grow. (All the companies in the AFC universe are growing; otherwise they wouldn't be included.) Growing companies earn more money. They pay out more cash as dividends. They plow back a growing stream of earnings into their businesses, thus enhancing the value of those businesses. This explains why stock prices *always* go up in the long run. The Dow Jones industrial average, the most famous measure of stock prices, rose from 88 in 1912 to more than 3700 by the end of 1993. That's from price appreciation alone and excludes cash dividends.

Some time ago, H. Bradlee Perry, chairman of the David L. Babson investment counseling firm, neatly summed up investing in stocks this way: "In the long run the price of just about every individual stock and the market value of all stocks together are determined by the growth of earnings and dividends. This is so simple that many of the sophisticated people in our [investing] field seem to overlook it. That is too bad because it does provide the basis for a very sound and unworrisome investment approach.

"Over the span of many decades corporate profits and dividends have trended upward in all industrial nations because their economies have expanded, not without business cycle interruptions of course, but in an inexorable trend of long-term growth."

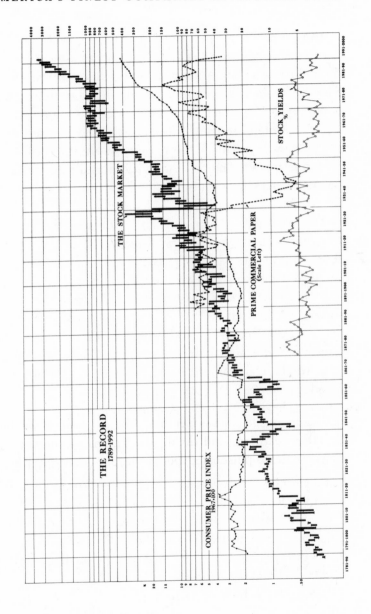

You can participate in America's future growth by owning shares of common stock in a variety of businesses even if they're not among America's Finest. But with America's Finest Companies, you're assured their businesses will continue to thrive and increase in value. As they do, so will the value of the stocks themselves and the cash dividends they pay. This is the reason you want to own your part of corporate America through America's Finest Companies. Stocks have outperformed all other investments for two hundred years.

The great patriot Patrick Henry addressed the Virginia Convention in 1775: "I know of no way of judging of the future but by the past." The past is important to investors because it gives us a picture of the future returns we can expect from various investments. The point I stress throughout this book is that stocks have always outperformed everything else, and America's Finest Companies have outperformed most other stocks. That being true, why would you want to invest your money in anything besides America's Finest Companies?

The scholarly *Financial Analysts Journal* published an article by Jeremy J. Siegel in its January-February 1992 issue. He's studied a lot of investment history as I have, and here's what he discovered. "Over the period from 1802 through 1992, equity [stocks] has provided returns superior to those on fixed-income investments, gold or commodities. Most strikingly, the real rate of return [with inflation taken out] on equity held remarkably constant over this period while the real return on fixed-income assets declined dramatically."

Going back to 1802, this is what $1.00 would have grown to by the end of 1992 without taking taxes into account.

Stocks	$3,050,000.00
Short-term government bonds	$2,934.00
Long-term government bonds	$6,620.00
Gold	$13.40
Inflation	$11.80

Over 190 years, stocks grew to be worth 1,040 times as much as short-term government bonds, 461 times as much as long-term government bonds, and astonishingly 227,612 times as much as gold. Stocks also came out 258,475 times ahead of inflation.

The obvious conclusion is—stocks knocked the socks off bonds and other fixed-income investments like savings accounts, money-market funds, and certificates of deposit. Since 1926 (the first year of Standard & Poor's stock price index), the compound annual return of all stocks listed on the NYSE, after subtracting inflation, was 6.4 percent compared with only 0.5 percent for Treasury bills. To say it another way, money invested in T-bills or ordinary savings accounts would have taken 139 years to double compared to only 11 years in stocks. America's Finest Companies work even faster.

Speaking of inflation, over every thirty-year period from 1802 through 1992, there were only two when the annual total return from stocks wasn't at least 3.5 percentage points ahead of the consumer price index. They occurred in the Great Depression. Highest real (after inflation is deducted) returns were in the 1960s and outdistanced inflation by more than 10 percentage points.

At this point, I bet I know what you're thinking: Everybody knows how well real estate has done. That's where all the great fortunes are made. Wrong! I'm going to talk about real estate and pop one of the great investing bubbles. Despite what you think or have heard or read, real estate is not as good as stocks.

The Harris Bank of Chicago analyzed returns from seven assets over three periods of time covering nearly one hundred years. I converted their data into the table on page 31 and updated it through 1985. Stocks were the hands-down winner all three times.

Stocks, after inflation was removed, earned a 6.0 to 6.9 percent compound annual return, far ahead of any of the other investments including farmland and housing.

If you want to take a look at more recent investment history—the past twenty-, ten-, five-, and one-year periods, the table from *Forbes* on page 32 will do nicely.

Through all the ups and downs of these periods, stocks leaped well ahead of all other investment categories, including real estate. Eight different assets outpaced the Consumer Price Index for the last two decades. Stocks were solidly in first place, with bonds and collectible stamps a distant second and third.

For the past ten years, stocks were again in first place, although bonds gave them a run for the money. Chinese ceramics (how do you invest in those?) were third but provided only half the return of stocks. Silver came in last, as it also did in the twenty-year time frame.

For the last five years, stocks were also in first place (this is getting repetitive), again followed closely by bonds. Only three other assets beat inflation as measured by the CPI, Consumer Price Index—Chinese ceramics, three-month Treasury bills, and diamonds. Housing and farmland both lagged the CPI.

During the latest twelve months, bonds beat stocks by 3.2 percentage points. Of the four periods shown, this is

REAL RETURNS ON INVESTMENT ASSETS
(ANNUAL RETURNS WITH INFLATION REMOVED)

	HOUSING	FARMLAND	GOLD	SILVER	COMMERCIAL PAPER	BONDS	STOCKS
1890–1985	4.8%	N.A.	(0.3)%	(1.9)%	1.8%	1.5%	6.2%
1912–1985	4.7	4.5%	(0.5)	0.1	1.1	1.0	6.0
1950–1985	4.6	6.5	2.2	1.9	1.7	(0.2)	6.9

INVESTMENT CLUES FROM THE PAST

ASSET	20 YEARS		10 YEARS		5 YEARS		1 YEAR	
	RETURN	RANK	RETURN	RANK	RETURN	RANK	RETURN	RANK
Stocks	12.2%	1	14.8%	1	15.1%	1	11.6%	2
Bonds	9.8	2	13.2	2	13.1	2	14.8	1
Stamps	9.6	3	(1.7)	11	0.5	11	8.8	4
3-month Treasury bills	8.8	4	7.3	4	6.6	4	3.3	8
Diamonds	8.5	5	5.9	5	4.3	5	1.5	11
Oil	7.5	6	(4.7)	12	1.7	9	(6.3)	12
Gold	6.9	7	(1.0)	9	(4.2)	12	9.6	3
Housing	6.7	8	4.4	7	3.7	7	1.8	10
CONSUMER PRICE INDEX	6.1	9	3.8	8	4.2	6	3.3	7
Chinese ceramics	5.8	10	7.6	3	9.8	3	(7.5)	13
U.S. farmland	5.4	11	(1.2)	10	2.1	8	2.3	9
Foreign exchange	3.4	12	5.6	6	1.7	10	6.2	6
Silver	2.7	13	(10.1)	13	(8.5)	13	8.4	5

Sources: Salomon Brothers Inc.; Diamonds, The Diamond Registry; Basket of U.S. stamps, Scott Inc.; Chinese ceramics, Sotheby's; Oil, American Petroleum Institute; Housing, National Association of Realtors; Farmland (excluding income), U.S. government statistics.
Note: Old Masters were excluded because current data were unavailable.

the only one in which stocks failed to top the list. But coming in second just one of four times isn't bad.

Will stocks do as well in the future as they have in the past? Will they remain the number-one investment? History resoundingly says the answer is "yes." Every long-term study I've ever seen says that, given enough time, stocks will be the best investment.

Given that stocks offer the best return on investment compared to anything else, why are certificates of deposit and money-market funds so popular today, especially in tax-deferred retirement plans? I think the answer must be because the principal is considered safe. With a CD, people know exactly what their rate of return is going to be. A money-market fund doesn't earn a guaranteed rate, but it is easy to get into and out of, and the return can be closely estimated in three- and six-month periods. Unfortunately, the vast majority of people mistakenly perceive that returns from stocks are wildly uncertain. That is not true except over very short periods of time.

George F. Baker, founder of First National Bank of New York (the forerunner of Citicorp), said that patience is one of three prerequisites for making a fortune in stocks. He knew time is on the side of the investor. He also knew that the longer you invest the better your results will be. History proves it. The table on page 34 spans nearly seven decades.

By analyzing the one-year periods we find that 29 percent of the time stocks earned a negative return. Their total return, price appreciation plus dividends, was a minus figure between January 1 of one year and January 1 the next. This is the number the Doubting Thomases cling to. They say, "Bill, in any given year the odds are

BUY SHARES OF AMERICA'S FINEST COMPANIES AND HOLD THEM. THE LONGER, THE BETTER.
(1926–1993)

	1 YEAR	5 YEARS	10 YEARS	20 YEARS
Holding periods (years from 1926)	68	64	59	49
Times outpacing inflation	46 (68%)	50 (78%)	52 (88%)	49 (100%)
Times with positive returns	48 (71%)	57 (89%)	57 (97%)	49 (100%)
Times with negative returns	20 (29%)	7 (11%)	2 (3%)	0 (0%)

Copyright © 1994 The Financial Training Group.

about one in three that share prices will decline. I can't run the risk of having my portfolio fall in value."

This retort may be true if you're sixty-five or seventy-five, but what if you're twenty-five or thirty-five? You have some thirty to forty years before you retire. Since investing is all about saving for the future—putting something aside today for tomorrow—time is on your side. Even if stock prices fall one or two years in a row, as long as you keep adding to your portfolio, you're going to do extremely well. Share prices of America's Finest Companies always recover. And then they move on to new highs.

Now take a look at the five-year segments. You can see that 89 percent of the time stock prices earned positive returns. Seventy-eight percent of the time they beat inflation, too. Only 11 percent of the time were they negative.

Going into the ten-year segments, stocks were negative just 3 percent of the time. All the remainder they were positive, and 88 percent of the time they outdistanced inflation as well.

By extending the investment period to fifteen or twenty years, the investor is guaranteed a profit, assuming as I do that history will continue to repeat. There was not a single fifteen-year stretch since 1926 when an investor with a diversified portfolio of good-quality stocks lost money. Not one. That's even better than housing. Far too many people think real estate prices never fall. This is not true. The price of an average single-family home plunged 40 percent between the mid-1920s and the mid-1930s. Housing prices did not reach their 1925 peak until 1948, twenty-three years after. Yes, investing in stocks really can be risk free if you are patient.

History is the only guide investors have for the future. History shows that CD and money-market investments barely keep ahead of inflation. Their future rate of return, after taking out inflation, will likely approximate the historic returns from commercial paper and bonds shown in the table on page 31, about 1.5 percent per year. At that rate it will take forty-seven years for money to double. But if an investor's money is in a balanced stock portfolio, it will grow at 6 to 7 percent per year (after inflation) and double in eleven to twelve years, four times as fast. In America's Finest Companies it will double even faster. I'll talk about how fast in Chapter 7.

Like commercial paper and bonds, gold and silver have been and should continue to be poor places for money. Housing and farmland ought to generate nice returns in the future as they have in the past but not nearly as great as the returns from common stocks.

No one knows what the future return from common stocks will be, or the inflation rate. If I were to guess, and I will, I'd say stocks—over the next thirty, forty, fifty, or sixty years—will grow at 10 to 12 percent annually, with inflation in the 3–4 percent range. Why is this important to know? Because if stocks and inflation continue to increase at their historic rates, you can project what a given amount of money today will be worth (with inflation taken out) in the future. You can also see what the miracle of compound interest does when you invest in America's Finest Companies.

Compounding can be traced back to the Babylonians. They were the original mathematicians, scientists, engineers, and financiers. Babylon is perhaps most famous for its hanging gardens. It was protected by a huge wall completely surrounding the city. Thousands of Babylonian writings on clay tablets have been discovered. Tables of compound growth, a law as secure as gravity, were among them.

Einstein considered compound interest to be humanity's greatest invention, since it allows for the systematic, reliable increase of wealth. Baron de Rothschild, when asked to name the seven wonders of the world, remarked, "I cannot. But I know that the eighth wonder is compound interest."

Sidney Homer, formerly with the investment-banking firm of Salomon Brothers, described the awesome benefits of compound interest this way: "$1,000 left to earn interest at 8% a year will be worth $23 quadrillion [$23,000,000,000,000,000] in 400 years, but the first hundred years are the hardest."

CHAPTER THREE

Valuable Lessons from Benjamin Graham

To achieve satisfactory investment results is easier than most people realize.

The typical individual investor has a great advantage over the large institutions.

—BENJAMIN GRAHAM

As stock prices fell relentlessly, day after day, week after week (I was so depressed it often seemed second after second) in the savage bear market of 1973–74, I was beginning to think I'd entered the wrong profession. What good was it being a Wharton-trained securities analyst when all my stock recommendations were getting clobbered?

When the Great Bear finally went into hibernation in fall 1974, I'd been in the securities profession exactly three years and three months. By that time, I'd been named "coordinator" of my firm's research efforts. I thought "coordinator" was a strange title, but it was better than nothing and at least it meant I was in charge. Shortly after being appointed to that role, I was made an officer and research director.

Between January 1973 and December 1974, the Dow Jones industrial average, the most popular stock-price index, plunged 45 percent. Only two other drops since World War I had been worse. One was during the Great Depression. The Dow reached 381 in 1929. By the end of 1932 it had gotten as low as 41, an 89 percent fall, nearly twice as deep as 1973–74. The other was 1937–38, when the Dow declined 49 percent in a mini-depression.

The few stock recommendations I'd made up to that time had collapsed in value, along with everything else my fellow analysts had on the buy list. Looking back at the carnage was as painful to me as it must have been to all the South Floridians who saw what Hurricane Andrew did to where they used to live. My personal portfolio shed nearly 75 percent of its value, and I kept wondering how many millions, if not hundreds of millions, of dollars my company's customers had lost.

I tend to bounce back quickly, so rather than dwell on what had gone wrong, as research chief I began to search for a method, any method, that would prevent the devastating losses of 1973–74 from ever afflicting me or any of my clients in the future. I was working on my chartered financial analyst certification, which would take other analysts three years to complete. Not me. I used four because I really enjoyed giving up a beautiful Saturday each June to endure a six-hour marathon exam.

I discovered that some years earlier the CFA program had used a different book from the one I'd been studying; it was *Security Analysis*, by Benjamin Graham and David Dodd. A third author, Sydney Cottle, was a later contributor. This bible of security analysts was originally published in 1934 shortly after the worst stock collapse in U.S. history ended.

The third edition, which I own, was essentially a rewriting rather than a revision of the original. When it came out in 1951, Benjamin Graham was president of the Graham-Newman Corporation, a money-management operation, and guest professor at Columbia University's graduate school of business. His collaborator and colleague, David L. Dodd, was a professor of finance there. What struck me about this particular edition was that it was dedicated to what the authors termed the "New Generation of Security Analysts." I'll never be able to ask either Graham or Dodd what they meant, but I suppose they were thinking World War II had escorted in a new era, both for the economy and for analyzing stocks and other securities. Their revised version was meant to educate a new breed of analysts and get them off on the proper footing.

Benjamin Graham is called the principal author of the five editions of *Security Analysis*. When he died in Aix-en-Provence in 1976 at age eighty-two, he was a millionaire. The dean of security analysts had sold more than

100,000 copies of his book before his passing. That's quite a large total for any book, especially a textbook.

Graham, born in 1894, grew up in New York, where he received his bachelor of science degree from Columbia in 1914. On graduating Phi Beta Kappa, Graham went to work on Wall Street. His first job was chalking up stock and bond prices on a board. From that lowly position he became a runner who delivered securities and checks, then on to assistant of a two-man bond department, where he wrote concise descriptions of the bonds in inventory to be sold. He also began writing a daily market letter.

Ben Graham was so proficient and got along so well with people he soon became a customers' man and personally visited customers as a bond salesman. A salesman he wasn't but a quick study he was. Young Graham soon realized how little his firm's customers really knew about the bonds they were buying and selling. He was later named a partner in the Wall Street firm of Newburger, Henderson & Loeb.

During the roaring bull market of the 1920s, Graham and Jerome Newman formed the Graham-Newman Corporation and an investment partnership, Newman & Graham. Even though they were pummeled in the 1929–32 stock freefall, their partnership churned out impressive returns before they dissolved it in the 1950s. Ten thousand dollars invested in Graham-Newman in 1936 threw off about $2,100 per year in income for the next twenty years (roughly $42,000), and the original principal was repaid when it liquidated.

I've often joked that *Security Analysis* isn't called the "bible of the trade" for nothing. It's thick, it's not easy or fun reading, and far too many of the professionals who have read it ignore many of its basic principles, just as have most readers of the Bible, the world's best-selling book. The edition I studied was the fourth, which had further refinements over the previous three, but the guts of it were still the same. I bought a copy and began to trudge through it on my own time. "Trudge" is the right word because, as in medical textbooks, there was much to learn on each page. I absorbed many lessons from Benjamin Graham, including his famous margin-of-safety concept: buy when stock prices overall are undervalued or pick out specific issues with promising prospects that sell well below their intrinsic worth.

When Graham started on Wall Street, a formal method for establishing the true value of stocks and bonds was all but nonexistent. There were various theories about how to speculate successfully in stocks, but not much attention was paid to investing. Speculating was a game of sorts. Graham knew investing to be the opposite, that it could and should be scientific. He believed basic principles could be uncovered that would enable students of the trade to learn how to buy $1.00 of assets at far less than their true worth. If this could be done, he reasoned, it was possible to earn handsome profits because few, if any, others were approaching securities analysis from such a solid quantitative base.

Since he was a teacher by nature and profession, Graham wanted to make his scientific investing principles available to others. That strong desire led him to write the epic on how to analyze securities. Unfortunately, *Security Analysis* is so unwieldy it has never reached the masses of individual investors as Graham so fervently desired, and it has managed to bypass more than its fair share of Wall

Street's best. Although the tools for investment success are within its pages, Graham's techniques are so cumbersome the vast majority of people whom he wanted to benefit, even if they were interested, didn't have the time to, and could never, put them to work.

Even so, Benjamin Graham's works and his various interviews and research papers were tremendously interesting to me. I was absorbed by everything I could learn from and about this investment master. I was especially fascinated to discover that Graham's primary reason for continually perfecting his craft was to show how to invest safely and with as little effort as possible.

This passion to share the gospel of investing with anyone who would listen led him to write *The Intelligent Investor* in 1949. In the introduction of a later edition of the book, Graham made certain the reader knew he wasn't writing for those who liked high risk or spending lots of time on their portfolios. Right away he had my attention.

Instead, *The Intelligent Investor* was dedicated to the defensive or passive investor who wanted to avoid large losses and the hassle of worrying about his investment strategy. Graham observed that the investor's worst enemy is himself or herself: "We have seen much more money made and *kept* by 'ordinary people' who were temperamentally well suited for the investment process than by those who lacked this quality, even though they had an extensive knowledge of finance, accounting, and stock-market lore." He made another astute observation: "Sound investment principles produced generally sound results."

By the time Graham was in his eighties, still as sharp as ever, financial institutions—brokerage firms, banks, insurance companies, and the like—were spending millions of dollars a year and grinding out thousands of pages of research on this or that security. This was the opposite of what was occurring when Ben Graham had stepped onto Wall Street some fifty years earlier. Little time or effort was then exerted on practical securities research. The kind of in-depth analysis Graham pioneered paid off handsomely, since there was virtually no competition.

As he grew older, Graham realized hordes of others were attempting to follow in his giant footsteps, so many in fact that they were bumping into one another while trying to pick undervalued securities—especially stocks—that would rise in value. He thought that since Wall Street was pouring such vast resources into stock research, the elaborate techniques he devised were rapidly losing their value. It seemed to be a case of what everybody else knows isn't worth knowing.

Graham communicated this view shortly before his death in 1976 in his final interview, which appeared in the September-October 1976 *Financial Analysts Journal.* Only one person in the United States is customarily introduced with no introduction—the President. Benjamin Graham was introduced almost as reverently as one "who needs no introduction to the readers of this magazine." Excerpts from that last interview appear here.

In the light of your sixty-odd years of experience in Wall Street, what is your overall view of common stocks?

Common stocks have one important investment characteristic and one important speculative characteristic. Their investment value and average market price tend to increase irregularly but persistently over the decades, as their net worth builds up through the reinvestment of undistributed earnings. However, most of the time common stocks are subject to irrational and excessive price fluctuations in both directions, as the consequence of the ingrained tendency of most people to speculate or gamble —i.e., to give way to hope, fear and greed.

What is your view of the financial community as a whole?

Most of the stockbrokers, financial analysts, investment advisers, etc., are above average in intelligence, business honesty and sincerity. But they lack adequate experience with all types of security markets and an overall understanding of common stocks—of what I call "the nature of the beast." They tend to take the market and themselves too seriously. They spend a large part of their time trying, valiantly and ineffectively, to do things they can't do well.

What sort of things, for example?

To forecast short- or long-term changes in the economy, and in the price level of common stocks, to select the most promising industry groups and individual issues—generally for the near-term future.

Can the average manager of institutional funds obtain better results than the Dow Jones Industrial Average or the Standard & Poor's Index over the years?

No. In effect, that would mean that the stock market experts as a whole could best themselves—a logical contradiction.

Turning now to individual investors, do you think that they are at a disadvantage compared with the institutions, because of the latter's huge resources, superior facilities for obtaining information, etc.?

On the contrary, the typical individual investor has a great advantage over the large institutions.

What general rules would you offer the individual investor for his investment policy over the years?

Let me suggest three such rules: (1) The individual investor should act consistently as an investor and not as a speculator. (2) The investor should have a definite selling policy for all his common stock commitments, corresponding to his buying techniques. (3) Finally, the investor should always have a minimum percentage of his total portfolio in common stocks and a minimum percentage in bond equivalents.

In selecting the common stock portfolio, do you advise careful study of and selectivity among individual issues?

In general, no. I am no longer an advocate of elaborate techniques of security analysis in order to find superior value opportunities. This was a rewarding activity, say, 40 years ago, when our textbook "Graham and Dodd" was first published; but the situation has changed a good deal since then. In the old days any well-trained security analyst could do a good professional job of selecting undervalued issues through detailed studies; but in the light of the enormous amount of research now being carried on, I doubt whether in most cases such extensive efforts will generate sufficiently superior selections to justify their cost.

In addressing the question about how individuals should create and manage their common-stock portfolios, Graham gave the two specific methods he preferred, both of which require a good deal of work on the part of the

individual. He followed by saying that "to enjoy a reasonable chance for continued better-than-average results, the
investor must follow policies which are (1) inherently
sound and promising, and (2) are not popular in Wall
Street," and "Investment is most intelligent when it is
most businesslike."

In addition to margin-of-safety, the cornerstone of the
Benjamin Graham philosophy of investing, these are the
other valuable lessons I learned from him:

1. Stock prices rise "irregularly but persistently" over
    time because the value of the underlying busi-
    nesses continues to increase as retained earnings
    are plowed back into those businesses.

2. Financial professionals, on the whole, are well edu-
    cated, honest, and sincere but have a shallow un-
    derstanding of common stocks.

3. Professionals spend far too much time trying to do
    what can't be done—predicting the future of the
    economy, the level of stock prices, and which in-
    dustries and individual stocks will perform best.

4. The average professional money manager cannot
    beat the market as measured by the Dow Jones in-
    dustrials, Standard & Poor's 500, or some other
    principal index. Professionals are the average, and
    it's a "logical contradiction" that they can "best
    themselves."

5. Individuals have tremendous advantages over the
    professionals.

6. In order to be most successful, individual investors
    (a) must invest rather than speculate, (b) have a

rule of thumb for the appropriate time to sell, and
(c) always have at least a minimum of their portfolios in stocks.

7. Complicated techniques of security analysis aren't
    necessary to unearth superior opportunities.

8. The stock-picking method an investor uses should
    be rational and easy to apply and have "an excellent
    supporting record." Investment that is most "busi-
    nesslike" will generate the best returns, especially
    when it goes against the grain of Wall Street.

By investing in America's Finest Companies the way
I'll detail, you'll be aligning yourself with the investment
wisdom and success of Benjamin Graham, the father of
security analysis and a multimillionaire when he died. I
can't say for certain whether Ben Graham would endorse
my techniques, but I strongly believe he would. They
meet all the criteria outlined in his farewell interview.
They are time-proven and they work. What else could an
investor want?

CHAPTER FOUR

Investing in America's Finest Companies Is the Simplest Way to Make Above-Average Profits

The simpler your investment plan, the more likely it will work.

— *U.S. NEWS & WORLD REPORT*

A simple investment program—one that is uncomplicated, readily understood, and easily implemented—is best because it's efficient. Simple investing will work very well for you, as it does for me and other knowledgeable investors. Garfield Drew, a noted stock-market technician (one who charts market and individual stock patterns as a guide to the future) of the 1950s, stated, "Simplicity or singleness of approach is a greatly underestimated factor of market success."

When people think of investing, simplicity is the last thing they think of. Everyone knows that investing (setting aside money today for the future) is a complex chore and not any fun either, right? Fun is not mentioned in investment books, courses in securities analysis, or investment letters (except mine). It should be. Having fun while you invest is critical to success. My strong belief is that if investing in stocks isn't fun for you, it won't be nearly as profitable as it can be.

Even if investing is profitable but you're not having fun (you constantly worry about day-to-day fluctuations in stock prices, or what you heard on *Wall Street Week*, or what the Federal Reserve did with the money supply, or the direction of the economy, or which way inflation and interest rates will go, or that the fifteen newsletters you subscribe to render conflicting advice, or ABC News says we're on the brink of recession, or some of the above or all of the above), you should try a new strategy.

The one I'm unfurling here is a good one. It's simple. It's rational. It produces superior results. It's fun. And it will beat most professional money managers year in and year out. My method is too simple for Wall Street to adopt, so they ignore it.

Benjamin Graham was asked in 1976 whether he recommended "careful study of and selectivity among individual issues." He responded, "In general, no. I am no longer an advocate of elaborate techniques of security analysis in order to find superior value opportunities."

My own studies dating back to the early 1920s confirm

exactly what Graham said. The more complicated your stock-market strategy, the more difficult it is to implement and to monitor. What's worse, it almost always leads to mediocre performance. Simple is far better. The pros make investing complicated, but it doesn't have to be.

If you think about it for fifteen seconds, you readily see why investment counselors, financial advisors, stockbrokers and money managers at banks, insurance companies, and mutual funds rarely beat the market indexes. Even those professionals who try to duplicate the market's results almost always fail. Here's why.

The Dow Jones industrials and Standard & Poor's 500 have no operating expenses. They go up and down without transaction costs. The money manager, trying to make his portfolio match one or the other market index, has to make frequent buys and sells to keep his portfolio in proportion with the stocks that make up the index he's working so hard to match. Stocks cost money to buy. They cost money to sell. The costs of trading, by themselves, make attempts to equal a market index virtually impossible.

If he's trying to beat the market instead of just equal it, the money manager has another dilemma. He usually cannot adopt a fun, businesslike, simple approach to investing like the one within these pages. Why? Because he (or she) wouldn't have to work a forty-hour week. He'd be taking so much time off, yet beating the indexes consistently, his boss would fire him. How could a company justify paying a money manager a full year's salary when he didn't have to work every day to profitably execute his investment plan?

The prudent money manager—one who wishes to remain employed—must create activities to fill his time. These include reading voluminous industry and company reports, dining with the management of companies he owns or might like to own, attending numerous presentations to security analysts and portfolio managers, talking with friends in the business, sitting through an untold number of investment-committee meetings, scanning in-depth and ultra-thick computer runs, plus listening to the latest Wall Street gossip.

By doing all these things and more, the typical money manager's day is out of his control. He drowns in wasteful short-term activities, which history shows don't produce above-average results. Yet he generally cannot quit because he can't afford to lose his salary. If you were in his shoes, would you be any different?

Fortunately, you don't have to get sucked into the rut of the typical money manager. You can go your own profitable way. And you'll start by buying only the shares of highest-quality companies, America's Finest. You won't learn that in other investment books. They dwell on this method or that for picking the next Wal-Mart, Home Depot, or other company that is sure to make a million dollars for you from a small amount of money. The reason these books generally aren't worth much, besides being hard to understand, is they focus on the wrong things. Choosing the "right" stocks for your portfolio is less important than any other step for stock-market success.

Of course you do have to pick companies for your portfolio. There are two characteristics to look for when you invest in shares of companies:

1. The companies are in sound financial condition and won't go out of business.
2. Earnings and dividends will continue to grow.

Where are these companies? You can go out and uncover them on your own. That's the harder way, but it can be interesting to do the research. Or you can do it the easier way and pick from the alphabetical list in the appendix.

If you'll turn to the list for just a moment and skim quickly through it, you'll see there are a lot of companies that are household words. One is Coca-Cola, perhaps the most famous name in the world.

Ten of the thirty Dow industrials are among America's Finest Companies. Coca-Cola is one. Another is Procter & Gamble, one of the world's premier consumer-products companies. Merck is a major pharmaceutical firm, while McDonald's sells more hamburgers (and owns more commercial real estate) than any other company in America. The other six are DuPont, Exxon, General Electric, Minnesota Mining & Manufacturing, J. P. Morgan, and Philip Morris.

When you invest your money, you want it to be 100 percent safe. Will Rogers used to say, "Forget about a return ON my investment. What I want is a return OF my investment." When you buy shares of America's Finest Companies, you are 99.9 percent guaranteed they'll remain in business. By investing in them exclusively, you know they will stay afloat in the worst economic storms.

Benjamin Graham believed in buying quality. In *The Intelligent Investor* he noted, "The risk of paying too high a price for good-quality stocks—while a real one—is not the chief hazard confronting the average buyer of securities. Observations over many years has taught us that the chief losses to investors come from the purchase of low-quality securities at times of favorable business conditions."

There are dozens and dozens of U.S. companies that have been around for well over a hundred years. Quite a few are among America's Finest Companies. They've survived panics, financial crises, depressions, earthquakes, droughts, floods, political scandals, wars, and any other disaster you can name. Among these are "blue-chip" companies such as Colgate-Palmolive, J. P. Morgan, and American Brands. They've been through just about everything, yet are still healthy and growing.

"Blue chip" describes highly regarded enterprises that generally make up the Dow Jones industrial average and a large part of the S & P 500. Blue chips have long earnings and dividend histories and are assumed to be able to withstand the most adverse economic circumstances.

Not all the companies included in America's Finest Companies are blue chips by the widely accepted definition, but they are all highly regarded and have exceptional records—at least ten consecutive years of higher earnings and/or dividends per share. As a group, they are well above average in financial strength. They are the thoroughbreds of corporate America and should be on the shopping list for assembling your personal market-beating portfolio.

The America's Finest Companies list comprises the top 3 percent (417) of all U.S. public companies. How have they been able to string together at least ten years in a row of higher earnings or dividends per share when the other 97 percent of public companies have not? Have a lot of them gotten into industries that are so good it would be hard not to be superachievers, or have most of them just been lucky? Or are there other factors? Is it possible to find some common threads that tie this elite group of companies together?

In the next few pages, you'll learn about four of America's Finest Companies, each of which is in a different industry. You may be unfamiliar with all of them, or perhaps you've heard of at least one. The first is the subject of a book written by a former CEO of the company. The second has the best earnings and dividend record in the banking industry and third-best in the AFC universe. The third company is one of the largest filtration companies in the world. The fourth is the second-largest user of recycled wastepaper in the United States.

AMERICAN BUSINESS PRODUCTS

Like many of the other companies in America's Finest Companies, American Business Products has a long heritage, with roots stretching back to St. Paul, Minnesota, in 1881. Henry Russell Curtis, the founder, was forced to resign from West Point in his third year over a hazing incident. He landed his first job, as a civil engineer, with the Union Pacific Railroad. When the line was extended to Denver, the project stalled, and Curtis had to look elsewhere for employment. Not wanting to be supported by his father, an Illinois attorney, he moved to St. Paul.

His first job there was selling unprinted stationery for cash commissions, and Henry Russell Curtis had to do his own collecting. He earned about $1.25 a day on average. One day he received an order for one thousand printed note-heads. This led to taking orders for printing and having a printer friend complete the assignment. There wasn't enough profit having another printer involved, so Curtis began his own small operation. One of his first big orders was for one thousand printed gummed labels for a local pharmacist.

By 1883, competition in the printing business was keener than ever. To further build his tiny business, Curtis began traveling to towns around St. Paul, which usually did not have a local printer and, even better, rarely had a printing salesman call. Being an astute businessman, Henry Russell Curtis followed one of the cardinal rules America's Finest Companies adhere to. He plowed every extra dime into his business.

In 1884, his wife, Mig, bore a stillborn daughter. Because Mig was so sickly, Curtis faced a crisis trying to keep his business prospering and paying for servants to help her, too. Two years later he declared bankruptcy. When his printing assets were sold, his father was the only bidder. Using money borrowed from his father, Curtis paid his creditors 25 percent cash and gave unsecured five-year notes for the other 75 percent.

Curtis Printing Company incorporated in the fall of 1886 with capital stock of $1,500, $100 per share. Henry Curtis owned thirteen shares, his wife one, and his son, Osborn, the other. That year the company had sales of $4,322. Volume nearly doubled the following year. In 1889 sales crossed the $10,000 mark for the first time, allowing a profit of nearly $1,000. The next year the company leaped into a new market—magazine binding.

The Great Depression of 1893 had lasting effects on large and small businesses for years. Throughout the nineties the company struggled to stay afloat. In 1901 the fledgling company adopted its first mission statement: "We ourselves carry only the BEST of everything, but can get for our customers anything else they want." (Note the strong emphasis on meeting customer needs.) Business was on the upswing. For the twelve months ended April 30, 1902, sales topped $30,000. Even better, the company was steadily improving the bottom line.

In the early 1900s, businesses used unattractive heavy-duty mailing envelopes made from manila or kraft paper. When they were filled, or overfilled as they often were, they were difficult to seal and, even worse, unattractive on arrival. Henry Russell Curtis experimented with all kinds of papers and designs to come up with a new, improved envelope. Out of his intense efforts came a revolutionary envelope made in Norway from the fibers of spruce and hemlock.

It was strong and flexible and had a special glue that improved the sealing. With a larger flap, it had more than three times the capacity of competitive envelopes of similar size. One of the company's early ads shows two men testing "Curtis Fibre" envelopes. It reads, "Have you tested your strength against Curtis Fibre? They can't pull it apart. See if you can. Samples gladly submitted for tests." Close to a century later, the company made another revolutionary envelope material, DuPont's Tyvek, a best-seller also.

With one major success under his belt, Curtis came up with a new-size envelope, a $10\frac{1}{2}$, which was the same length as a standard number 10 and the same depth as the number 11. Measuring 4½ by 9½ inches, it fit well into a regular typewriter but had an extra-deep flap with special gumming. By making the new envelope from his special fiber, Curtis gave birth to the Curtis Fibre Envelope, which filled a tremendous need for major users of extra-duty envelopes. The company moved into a new building in 1913 at 1000 University Avenue. Curtis put up a large sign, "Curtis, 1000," and found it was easy for everyone to remember. In later years, the name Curtis 1000 was heavily promoted and advertised and is still in use today.

Henry Russell Curtis died of a heart attack on a cruise around the world in 1927. His son, Henry, began running the company, and Henry's wife joined the small board of directors. It was uncommon to have a woman in a company, either as a senior executive or director, but Henry Curtis wasn't worried. "She will bring into our directors' meeting a woman's intuition and she has brains." Apparently, Curtis 1000 was one of the first American companies to recognize business skills of women.

The grandson of Henry Russell Curtis, Harry, was the founding chairman and president of American Business Products, successor to Curtis 1000. Curtis 1000 is now a division of ABP, headquartered in Atlanta, and is a leading manufacturer and supplier of printed business forms, envelopes, business supplies, and books. The company is also engaged in specialty extrusion coatings and the laminating of papers, films, and nonwoven fabrics for the packaging industry. Roughly three-quarters of its sales are from business forms, envelopes, and specialty mailers. Its Curtis 1000 subsidiary is one of the country's largest direct marketers of business envelopes.

In 1969, American Business Products went public, with

200,000 shares sold at 17 per share, and was traded over the counter. A year later it acquired Atlanta Business Forms and Southwest Business Forms. BookCrafters, now BookCrafters USA, was organized in 1972 to operate the nation's first fully automated book-production plant. This unique system combined a belt press with bindery to produce a completed book in only one pass through the press. James Herriott's acclaimed *All Things Bright and Beautiful* was produced by BookCrafters in 1974. The first edition and twelve reprintings pumped more than 400,000 copies into circulation.

Continuing its growth-through-acquisition strategy, ABP brought Vanier Graphics Corporation into the fold in 1976. American Fiber-Velop Manufacturing followed four years later. In 1983, Curtis 1000 Europe GmbH was formed as a joint venture with a German company to produce and market Tyvek envelopes in Europe. Cascade Business Forms was purchased in 1989, followed by Jen-Coat, Inc., in 1990. ABP's European joint-venture company acquired Envelopes International in 1991, followed by Neuwieder Couvert Fabrik in 1992.

ABP's mission is "facilitating and enhancing business communications" through whatever form or forms that may take in the future. The company, right from its roots, has had the reputation of being state-of-the-art in its plants and equipment, so it can meet the demands of its customers. Management believes its ongoing acquisition program continually bolsters its product lines.

Through 1993, American Business Products enjoyed fifty-five straight years of higher sales and thirty-seven of higher dividends. Since the initial public offering in 1969, both sales and earnings increased fifteenfold. The company continues to thrive in good times and bad. How? Past Chairman Harry Curtis explains, "Looking back over a century of growth by the company, which my grandfather founded, I am struck by the predominance of certain values within the business itself. The striking thing is that these values have remained constant, unchanged by the dynamics of the business, the blows of the worst economic storms, the vagaries of politics, or the shifting sands of societal trends.

"These values are expressed in such words as quality and integrity of product, good service, 'a full count,' honesty and decency in business dealings, opportunity, creativity, respect, hard work, profits, and security.

"These principles . . . constitute the foundation stones of the business."

BANK OF GRANITE CORPORATION

If the name makes you think of a bank that's solid as a rock, that's what it's supposed to do. In fact, the 1992 annual report featured a huge color picture of—you guessed it—granite on the front cover. Even though few have heard of it or know where the headquarters is located (Granite Falls, North Carolina; population 3,200), Bank of Granite is a powerhouse of a company sporting the finest track record in banking and third-best among all public companies—forty straight years of higher earnings and dividends through 1993. Started in 1906, it has consistently been one of the most profitable institutions in banking and has knocked the socks off the stock market. One share purchased in 1954, when the present management came aboard, cost $211.55. Through numerous stock splits and dividends, that one share became 1,254 by June 30, 1993, and was worth $35,739. That's a compound 14.2 percent annual rate of appreciation and does not include dividends reinvested.

It's a hallmark of this smallish bank (slightly more than $300 million in deposits, fewer than two hundred employees, ten branches), in the words of CEO John Forlines, that "we often sacrifice growth for profitability and do not put much emphasis on size per se." The company never participated in the leveraged-buyout craze and has no foreign loans, no loans to Third World countries, and most important, "no loans on pork bellies." Forlines was once asked to describe a foreign loan. He jokingly replied, "It's a loan made outside our home county."

Taking care of business and sticking to what it knows best has made Bank of Granite the most profitable bank in the country for the past two years, according to *United States Banker*. The magazine reported Bank of Granite earned an average 2.09 percent on assets for each of the previous four years, more than twice the 1 percent level that is considered good performance. That's an especially remarkable feat given that the bank operates in just three counties in the Western Piedmont of the Tar Heel state. Forlines says there's "no burning secret, no smoking gun, no magic formula" to account for his bank's superior record. "It's just a lot of little things. We run a lean ship."

The bank has always exhibited a fierce independence, both in the ways it thinks and operates and in its strong intent not to be gobbled up by a larger bank. But Bank of Granite is anything but antiprogressive. It keeps up with the latest technologies and banking programs, making sure they add to, rather than detract from, the bottom line. Since 1954 it's been run by John Forlines, who credits hard work and tremendous people as the two ingredients that have made the bank so enormously successful. Executives from competing chain banks frequently don't stay very long in the area because they're biding their time waiting to be promoted. Bank of Granite's managers, on the other hand, rarely move. They like where they live, and they like where they work. They are woven through the fabric of the towns where they live and work.

Bank of Granite, with Forlines taking the lead, keeps a tight rein on costs. The corporation had only one branch office until 1960. About two decades ago there was some talk that nearby Wachovia Corporation would acquire the bank, but negotiations never got very far. There was a regulatory problem, for one thing, but Forlines realized he didn't want to go the way of the megabanks, even though Wachovia is one of the finest.

Interestingly, the company he might have merged with put him into business. Following World War II, Forlines, a graduate of Duke University, returned to Durham, North Carolina, where he went into the hardware and appliance business with his brother-in-law. He had been a teller at the Duke-campus branch of Citizens National Bank before the war and wanted to get back into banking. Friends at Wachovia introduced him to a group that owned Bank of Granite, a $1 million enterprise at the time, "whose fortunes had sagged" according to one newspaper's account.

Because of its size, Forlines has been able to make a big imprint on "his" bank. The company is so small it doesn't need a layer of middle managers. There wouldn't be anything for them to do. No one, not even the chairman, is a prima donna. Forlines answers his own phone when he's in. He's frugal and watches expenses as intently as a hungry lion stalks his next meal. He expects every bank employee to do the same. Even though he reads up to five newspapers per day, he pays for them, not the bank. He even had the lead hand in preparing the packet of materials I used to write this profile. Forlines scribbled notes to me in several places.

He would never think of "wasting" money on an outside public-relations department or one on the inside either. He even noted in the annual address to shareholders that almost all the 1992 annual report was done in-house on a Macintosh computer, thus "saving the bank a lot of money." Over and over again, from everything Bank of Granite says and does, it's obvious there are no extra people anywhere. The bank treats its customers' money with respect. Forline's office has a view unlike that of any other CEO I know—the railroad tracks.

Bank of Granite is so hugely successful and profitable because it believes in itself and its cause and works diligently in pursuit of the finest. This is clearly reflected in the closing paragraph of the 1990 annual report:

> As we enter our 85th year of dedicated "hometown" service, we do so with a sense of humility and gratitude to so many for helping us build a solid foundation. Uncertainty in the economy is nothing new. Over the years, Bank of Granite has seen prosperity and recession, inflation and disinflation, fuel shortages and gluts. We have experienced them all and every year earnings have increased. With the continued support of our friends, shareholders, customers, and employees, we are confident that we will

continue to meet new challenges and opportunities with the same enthusiasm and dedication that has served our bank so well for the past 85 years.

MILLIPORE CORPORATION

In its 1990 annual report, Millipore described itself this way:

> Millipore is a multinational growth company that leads the $3.2 billion separations industry with the broadest range of separations technologies and products available. These technologies and products are used for critical applications in a wide range of industries including the pharmaceutical, biotechnology, microelectronics, environmental, life science research, chemical, patient care, and food and beverage industries.
>
> Millipore succeeds through its strong focus on the customer, and its commitment to meeting or exceeding customer expectations for product quality, technical support, application knowledge, and ease of doing business.

The first paragraph is a mouthful, and it would still be easy not to understand what the company is all about after reading it. In plain English, Millipore breaks down, analyzes, and purifies fluids. Millipore helps the pharmaceutical industry maintain purity and quality in the manufacturing process and also in research and development activities. Millipore test kits quickly and easily detect the numerous pesticide residues in water, soil, and food. In the semiconductor industry, Millipore has developed innovative contamination-control products to meet the extremely high levels of manufacturing purity required.

Millipore analytical instruments, "membrane" devices, and/or manufacturing systems are in almost all biotechnology companies, a field with explosive growth potential.

The second paragraph is right to the point. Millipore is keyed to the customer and wants to do better for customers than customers expect. That's one trait America's Finest Companies have in common. Few companies spell it out so clearly.

Although earnings don't go up every year (they fell in 1989 and again in 1992), Millipore is a genuine growth company. Sales more than tripled to $777 million in 1992 from $254 million in 1981. Net profit, excluding nonrecurring items, climbed from just under $10 million in 1981 to nearly $55 million in 1991. Earnings dropped to $33.2 million the following year.

Millipore's sales break down into three parts: semipermeable membranes (about 38 percent), chromatography (roughly 55 percent), and other (7 percent). Membranes do exactly what they sound like they do—separate fluid components by size of the components. It's easy to see applications in health care and biotechnology for filtering all types of fluids and solutions to remove impurities and other undesirable substances. The trend toward miniaturization in microchips means the chemical solutions that wash and etch chips must be purged of micron-size contaminants. They're often so small they can only be seen with high-powered microscopes. Ditto for the beverage markets. They filter microorganisms out of the products. Kirin Brewery Company, which controls about 50 percent of the Japanese beer market, has a fully automated brewery, with Millipore purification products working throughout the plant.

In an area as simple-sounding as pure water, Millipore has become the leader. Distilled water is many times purer than drinking water. Water used in research laboratories is many times purer than that. Water is everywhere in a lab. It's used to wash things and to prepare chemical solutions and tissue cultures. Ultrapure water is required for in vitro fertilization and bacterial fermentation. Millipore has systems that produce pure water on demand, because stored water, even though purified, quickly becomes tainted.

The lab-water business has plenty of competition, so Millipore has to be creative to gain market share. Creativity is a hallmark of America's Finest Companies. Millipore has learned what to do to fill customers' needs by asking them, and then giving them what they want. Sounds easy, doesn't it? But asking the right questions and listening for answers is hard. Millipore has the necessary skill and continually hones it. That's what being one of the finest companies is all about.

As analytical instruments become more sensitive, water purity is even more important. According to Millipore, industry needs more-compact systems that are easier to use. As in the trend from mainframes to personal computers, scientists are shifting to small, modular, self-contained water systems and ditching the old, large ones because lab space is at a premium. This move saves space. Millipore's "intention is to continue to anticipate and respond" to needs. "Complete solutions—from tap to point-of-use—will be pursued."

Chromatography is the largest segment of Millipore's operation. It's a technique to isolate, analyze, and purify organic molecules, especially in the pharmaceutical area.

Picture a liquid streaming through a column of porous materials, which break it down into its various parts. A detector then analyzes each of the different components and sends the results to a computer for analysis. Liquid-chromatography systems must process the smallest samples as fast as they can at the lowest possible cost with maximum reliability. That's a lot to ask, but Millipore is able to deliver exactly what its customers need.

In his letter to shareholders in 1992's annual report, CEO John H. Gilmartin noted the company is heavily committed to protecting the environment. As part of the company's "Managing for Excellence" process, the company agreed to cut unsound emissions by 50 percent by 1995. When his letter was written, Millipore was already two years ahead of schedule. The company eliminated the use of ozone-depleting chemicals by the end of 1993. Packaging improvements have reduced solid waste, and the company has undertaken a "comprehensive grass roots approach to material and chemical substitutions that will further [its] environmental efforts."

With strong finances, secure world markets, and the best technology base in its history, Millipore is charting a path of above-average future growth.

SONOCO PRODUCTS COMPANY

On May 10, 1899, Major James Lide Coker formed the Southern Novelty Company in Hartsville, South Carolina (which isn't particularly close to any town you've heard of), to begin manufacturing paper cones as an economical alternative to the then-standard wooden cones used most commonly in textile mills to wrap thread around. The founder's grandson, James Coker, was president of the company in the 1930s, when he wrote down the company's philosophy of doing business: "To produce a product or service that fills the need better than any other product or service . . . a product that lives up to every expectancy of its user."

When the company was established, there were 1,000 shares authorized at $100 per share. Stock was offered to the public for the first time in 1937. Today there are nearly 88 million shares outstanding. An investor who purchased 100 shares of Sonoco in 1959 at 25 per share (a $2,500 total investment) would have nearly 10,000 shares today worth approximately $225,000. And that's excluding cash dividends paid for thirty-five years.

James Lide Coker attended the Citadel, a military college in Charleston. He topped that off by attending Harvard and studying under the zoologist Louis Agassiz. Returning home to Hartsville in 1858, he began work on his father's thousand-acre plantation, to which he was deeded half. Coker fought gallantly in the Civil War, was severely wounded, and came back to Hartsville from a Baltimore prison with a shattered hip. In the process of a long recovery, he opened a country store and helped found a bank, a cotton mill, and a college.

Coker's oldest son, James, wanted to build a paper-making facility in Hartsville because a research paper he'd written at Stevens Institute of Technology in New Jersey led him to believe paper pulp could be made there from the abundant shortleaf pine. Following construction of the mill around 1890, one failure followed another and the new company almost went into financial ruin. But by 1893 the pulp-making process had been refined enough so that a new Fourdrinier paper machine was built, at a cost of $19,500, to manufacture five to eight tons of paper per day. As a contrast, by the mid-1970s, eighty years later, a new paper machine cost $10 million and Sonoco turned out 1,700 tons of paper daily. The company's one Fourdrinier machine today has an annual capacity of 175,000 tons.

In 1900 the Southern Novelty Company had sales of $17,000 and earnings of $2,000. The textile industry thrived throughout the South and Sonoco along with it. Major Coker passed away in 1918 at age eighty-one and the reins were handed to his son, Charles. Sales that year were $514,000, net profit $34,709.

Charles Coker, the second CEO of the young growth company, died in 1931 at age fifty-two. Besides the main plant in Hartsville, another plant was acquired, in New Jersey, plus a joint venture begun in Manchester, England. By then, sales had grown to $1.6 million accompanied by net profit of $200,000. Charles Coker's son James, age twenty-seven, became the third president. His brother, Charles, twenty-five, was groomed for senior management.

James studied at the University of North Carolina and Harvard Business School. He was said to have "a rare combination of meticulous management skills and a gambler's flair for optimistic speculation." Under him, the firm began a rapid expansion to develop new product lines and faster production methods. Eight new plants were either started from scratch or purchased.

Following James Coker's death in 1961, younger brother Charles became the fourth president. At his request, he moved into the chairmanship in 1970, and his son Charles, whom I've known and admired for more than a decade, took over the helm as only the fifth president of a corporation that will soon be one hundred years old. The only company in America's Finest Companies with almost as few people at the top over such a long span is Wachovia Corporation in Winston-Salem, North Carolina, one of the country's most impressive banks from any number of standpoints. L. M. Baker is only the sixth person in the CEO slot.

Today, C. W. Coker, Jr., is chief executive officer of a company with more than $1.9 billion in sales and net earnings exceeding $118 million. The cover of the 1992 annual report boldly proclaims, "We will be a customer-focused, global packaging leader, recognized for superior quality and high-performance results. Integrity and a commitment to excellence will be the hallmark of our culture."

Sonoco Products has been ranked the fifth-largest domestic packaging company and tenth-largest in the world, yet few consumers or investors have ever heard of it. The company has a world-wide presence—twenty-four countries on five continents, two hundred operations, and sixteen thousand employees. Every year the company churns out hundreds of products, most of which are called carriers or containers—tubes, cores, cones, drums, cans, cartridges, plastic sacks, and more. Sonoco serves these industries: paper, paperboard, textiles, food and beverage, supermarkets, pharmaceuticals, business machines, construction, shipping, storage, plastics, and many others. Two-thirds of sales go for industrial uses, the rest for consumers.

Although no customer accounts for more than 2–3 percent of total sales, they are a Who's Who of industry—DuPont, Coca-Cola, Wal-Mart, and Georgia Pacific, to name four. You have used Sonoco's products frequently although you probably didn't know it. Ajax cleanser comes in a Sonoco package. So do Pringle's potato chips, Ovaltine, Kodak film, Chun King noodles, Mobil oil, and Ultra Slim Fast powders.

Sonoco is one of the world's major recyclers. About 90 percent of the products it turns out use recovered or recycled material. The company's papermaking operations around the world recycle more than one million tons of recovered paper each year. Internally, Sonoco recycles more than 120 million gallons of water per day and annually reclaims 16 million pounds of plastic. The company works closely with existing customers to find new and innovative ways to bring products to market at less cost and with less negative impact on the environment, a trademark of so many of America's Finest Companies.

What makes Sonoco one of America's Finest Companies? Certainly visionary and stable leadership has played a principal role. The company has had five able chief executives since its founding before the turn of the century. Major James Lide Coker began and ran the company for nineteen years. After his death, Charles W. Coker, the architect of Sonoco's early growth, was president for thirteen years. James Lide Coker III, a grandson of the founder, diversified the company outside the textile business. He remained president for three decades before his younger brother, Charles W. Coker, Sr., took his place in 1961. Sonoco saw its most dramatic growth during his tenure, which lasted from 1961 until 1976. Charles W. Coker, Jr., the present CEO, has guided the company into strategic markets throughout the world.

The safety of Sonoco's workers permeates almost everything I read about the company. Since 1982 injuries have been cut from 6.09 per 100 employees to 1.1 per 100 at the end of 1992. The company strongly believes even one worker injury per year is too much and is committed to a totally injury-free work environment. This goal of complete worker safety is part of Sonoco's goal to be a world-class competitor. According to a company brochure, "managers put safety at the top of the list," not profits. Company executives think safety is an essential measure of effective management. To prove it, company policy requires that the president of the company be alerted within sixty minutes of any injury.

Apart from astute leadership and the resoluteness to prevent any worker from being hurt, Sonoco Products' innovative product lines have fueled the company's growth and taken it to the forefront in many of its niche markets. For a large enterprise in *Fortune*'s top 250, the company acts like a much smaller animal. The company is a master at taking mature products like cores, tubes, and cones and continually finding new markets for them. It focuses on dominating mundane businesses by keeping costs low and driving them even lower.

At Sonoco, customers and employees are everything. That commitment has resulted in superior returns for investors. A thousand dollars invested in Sonoco Products at the end of 1983, with dividends reinvested, was worth $5,062 on December 31, 1993. That same thousand dollars in the Standard & Poor's 500 grew to just $4,020.

Having studied and analyzed hundreds of America's Finest Companies, I believe they share the following traits:

1. The finest companies serve customers and employees with a passion.
2. Their managements are strong and decisive.
3. Each company knows where it wants to go.
4. They carve out their own paths for growth.
5. The companies are creative and innovative.
6. They carefully control expenses.
7. They respond to problems rather than react to them.

If you invest exclusively in America's Finest Companies, you'll be putting these traits to work for you in your portfolio. If the historic performance of their stocks continues, you'll do far better than most professional money managers.

CHAPTER FIVE

Where Are the Customers' Yachts?

William R. Travers was a well-known nineteenth-century lawyer who regularly used to visit swank Newport, Rhode Island. J. P. Morgan, John D. Rockefeller, and other notable Wall Street financiers and millionaire industrialists built "cottages" (we call them mansions today) there for weekend and summer retreats. Yacht racing was the sport of that day, and Travers was present at all the best events. One Sunday he was in a small group at the finish line watching yacht after yacht glide across. As names of the owners were announced, Travers noticed each one was a wealthy stockbroker. While staring at the fancy flotilla, Travers, a stutterer, shouted out, "And w-w-where are the c-c-customers' yachts?"

Fred Schwed, Jr., wrote best-selling *Wacky, the Small Boy* in 1939. In the About the Author section, Schwed was said to have "attended Lawrenceville and Princeton and has spent the last ten years in Wall Street. As a result he knows everything there is to know about children." That doesn't say much about Schwed's forte in the financial arena, but it does give you a good idea of the terrific sense of humor he had. Schwed was an early skeptic of Wall Street and decided to write *Where Are the Customers' Yachts?* (or *A Good Hard Look at Wall Street*) to share his witty wisdom. He got Simon & Schuster to publish it in 1940. The book has been successful enough to have been reprinted several times since.

Schwed's opening reminds the reader that Wall Street has a river at one end and a graveyard at the other. Schwed said he viewed Wall Street's daily activities from a trading table with every conceivable form of communication except the heliograph. In such an enviable position, he was "constantly exchanging . . . quotations, orders, bluffs, fibs, lies and nonsense." Having observed all this for at least a decade, Schwed decided to dedicate his book to examining the nonsense, "a commodity which keeps sluicing in through the weeks and years with the irresistible constancy of the waters of the rolling Mississippi."

I particularly liked his discussion of investment trusts, which were the forerunners of modern-day mutual funds. They were formed under the assumption that

> the average individual is incapable of handling his own financial destiny. What is worse, he cannot, unless he is very rich, purchase the best financial advice. (We are assuming for the moment that there is such a thing as the best financial advice.)

So a lot of us who clearly are not magicians pool our

money and hire a set of professional experts to do the guessing. They may not be quite magicians but they have everything that should be necessary—experience, reputation, trained staffs, inside information, and unlimited resources for research. Since the amount we pool together is often in the neighborhood of a hundred million dollars, we can afford to pay them fortunes for their ability. Paying them fortunes will be a great bargain for us, provided only that they come across with the ability.

One would think they could do this, or at least do it better than we could. If investment trusts would only function in actuality anything like as well as they do in theory, they would be a tremendous asset to the general welfare.

Schwed believed most investment professionals aren't dishonest. They're simply inept. He wrote, "This book has chiefly tried to paint a picture of thousands of erring humans, of varying degrees of good will, solemnly engaged in the business of predicting the unpredictable. To this effort most of them bring a certain cockeyed sincerity." I agree with Schwed.

Since I started my newsletter, *Bill Staton's Money Advisory*, nine years ago, I've amassed a thick file of evidence that proves that the large majority of professional money managers, the experts millions of people rely upon to help their money grow, consistently underperform the stock market. The file is close to two inches thick and growing. It's jam-packed with articles from all sorts of places, but for the most part they're straight from everyday business and financial journals, including *The Wall Street Journal, Forbes, Fortune, Business Week,* and *Financial World*. I haven't gone out of my way to obtain the evidence. It comes regularly and frequently in my mail.

Here's a simple example. Each month *The Wall Street Journal* has four stock-picking experts recommend buying a stock or shorting (selling a stock in the hopes it will go down and the investor can buy it back at a lower price). After the four stocks are chosen, the *Journal* throws four darts to pick a portfolio of its own. Then the results are tracked during the next six months to see who did better. After a total of forty-four overlapping six-month contests (January to June, February to July, etc.), the experts are ahead, with twenty-six victories compared to eighteen for the darts. That's not very convincing proof that the professionals are worth the typical six-figure salaries so many of them command. Yes, these high-paid pros can afford to buy yachts. But can the customers they advise afford to do the same?

Before I explain why most professionals cannot beat the market on a regular basis, I want to show you some recent evidence of the poor job they're doing:

1. One might expect that our investment judgments, given our training and experience, would prove sound and profitable for our clients. But this is, strikingly, not true.

    —ARNOLD S. WOOD, PRESIDENT
    MARTINGALE ASSET MANAGEMENT
    FINANCIAL ANALYSTS JOURNAL, MAY–JUNE 1989

2. In the 10-year period ending December 1988, SEI, a pension fund consulting firm, found only 40 percent of all pension funds were able to beat the S & P 500 at least half the time. Only one manager in 100 beat the market in each of 10

years, and only one manager in 50 beat the market in each of five years.

—*THE FINANCIAL WEEKLY*, JANUARY 29, 1990

3. 75% of all professional money managers fail to beat the market in any given period, according to studies done by Ibbotson Associates of Chicago, an investment research firm.

—*FINANCIAL WORLD*, MAY 1, 1990

4. Since 1969, the unmanaged S & P 500-stock index has handily outgained the average stock fund, rising 680% vs. 550%. $10,000 invested on Jan. 1, 1969, in a portfolio that matched the S & P would have grown to $78,600 last Jan. 1. The same amount in the average stock fund: $65,800.

—*MONEY*, MAY 1991

5. Of the more than 1,000 equity mutual funds in existence, only a handful have beaten the market over the past 10 years.

—*THE MUTUAL FUND LETTER*, JULY 1991

6. Of the 41 domestic equity funds managed by Merrill Lynch, Shearson, Paine Webber, Dean Witter and Prudential Securities, only 2 have beaten the market since 1988. Over the period, not one of these five brokerage firm families outperformed the S & P 500.

—*FORBES*, SEPTEMBER 2, 1991

7. Many of the 400 or so investor newsletters aren't worth the price of a subscription, which can run $500 or more a year.

—*FORTUNE*, SEPTEMBER 23, 1991

8. Only four services [investment letters] outperformed the Wilshire 5000 over the $11\frac{1}{2}$ period [6/30/80–12/31/91], which shows you how tough it is to beat the market.

—*THE CHARTIST*, FEBRUARY 6, 1992

9. "About a fifth of the investment letter universe appears to beat the market over the long term," says Hulbert, pointing out that less than 20% of all mutual funds outperform the market.

—INTERVIEW WITH MARK HULBERT, PUBLISHER OF *HULBERT'S FINANCIAL DIGEST* IN *FORBES*, SEPTEMBER 14, 1992

10. The average stock mutual fund climbed just 7.89% in the year [1992] through Dec. 23, slightly behind the Standard & Poor's 500-Stock Index.

—*THE WALL STREET JOURNAL*, JANUARY 4, 1993

11. According to Lipper Analytical, stock funds returned 13.5% a year over the 10 years through December [1992], compared with 16.2% for the Standard & Poor's 500-Stock Index.

—*THE WALL STREET JOURNAL*, MARCH 5, 1993

12. By and large, professional investors do a mediocre job of stock-picking. That, along with their expenses and fees, causes them to lag well behind the market.

—*BUSINESS WEEK*, MAY 31, 1993

Mutual funds have become the most popular way for individuals to invest. There are now in excess of 5,000 different mutual funds, with more than $2 trillion in assets at the end of 1993. About 1,000+ of them invest in stocks. With so much money on the line and pouring into the equity funds at a record clip (over $128 billion in 1993), you'd think investors would be more careful about where they put their money. But they are often lured by the creative advertising of mutual funds, which seem to offer so much and in reality frequently produce so little. Thumb through any of dozens of investment publications, and you'll see ads for this fund or that. Note how they tout their "outstanding" records. One of my money-manager friends (who actually does beat the market) wryly noted, "Every money manager in the country says he's in the top 25 percent." But we know that's an impossibility.

If an investor is going to beat the market over the long term (I define long term as a minimum of ten years), he or she will have to invest strictly in funds that invest exclusively in stocks. The reason is that stocks have beaten all other investments, real estate included, for well over a century. I wanted to see how many equity mutual funds outpaced the market in the past decade, so I checked out the CDA/Wiesenberger Mutual Funds Update, which comes out monthly.

For the ten years through December 31, 1993, the Dow Jones industrial average provided a compound annual return of 15.7 percent, while the S & P 500 earned 14.9 percent. The Dow index is trackable well back into the nineteenth century, while the S & P 500, which got its start in 1926, measures the performance of five hundred different companies. These are the two benchmarks fund managers try to beat, but very few do.

CDA/Wiesenberger separates stock funds into various categories. Among funds for maximum capital gains, only five managed to beat the market for the past ten years. Small company growth funds had six market beaters, while international equity funds had eight. Long-term growth, growth and current income, balanced, and equity income funds together had fewer than twenty that bested the two major market indexes during the past decade.

These seven fund categories produced less than forty (out of more than 1,000) stock funds that performed better than the market since the end of 1983. That's about 4 percent, a small handful of winners.

Since so few professionals, whether they be investment counselors, pension-fund managers, or mutual-fund managers, beat the market, investors need to understand why so they don't make the same mistakes the pros make. Financial institutions control about 80 percent of all trading volume on the New York Stock Exchange. On an average day some 200 to 300 million shares are bought and sold. Individuals account for 20 percent of that.

Vilfredo Pareto was an Italian sociologist and economist for whom the famous Pareto Principle is named. After observing thousands of workers in hundreds of businesses from the late nineteenth through the early twentieth century, he concluded that 80 percent of results comes from 20 percent of effort. To say it another way, 20 percent of an advertising budget results in 80 percent of the incremental revenue. Twenty percent of a day's work produces 80 percent of the benefits of that work. The top 20 percent of workers in any organization typically produce about 80 percent of sales and earnings. Although no results will divide exactly into 20/80, it's an excellent rule of thumb. And it's interesting to me that NYSE volume is now almost exactly 20 percent by individuals and 80 percent by financial institutions. As you've already seen, the 80 percent produces subpar results, which implies the 20 percent, individual investors, produces superior results.

I profiled Benjamin Graham, the father of modern-day securities analysis, in Chapter 3 and provided excerpts from the final interview he gave shortly before his death. In just ten sentences, Graham ripped apart the fantasy that the financial community can accurately predict short-term changes in the economy and stock prices. He also reasoned that the stock-market experts can't continuously beat the market because they are the market. You can't beat the average when you are the average.

On the other hand, "The typical individual investor," he said later in the interview, "has a great advantage over the large institutions." As I'll demonstrate, that advantage can lead you to above-average profits if you create and manage your own portfolio made up of America's Finest Companies.

I don't want you to think I'm bashing all professional money managers and advisors. For the record, I am not against professional advice or money management. I *am* against paying a so-called expert for subpar performance, something far too many individuals are doing. In fairness to the pros, though, their customers help create these inferior results. Here's how.

For whatever reasons—lack of time, no investment background, personal finance seeming too complicated—many people believe they can't manage their own money well. Since they have no confidence in their own ability, they turn to experts to take care of their money for them. An expert is defined as one "displaying special skill or knowledge derived from training and experience." Millions of people believe there are a large number of stock-market experts who earn superior investment returns, primarily through accurate forecasting and making savvy moves into and out of stocks. Even though this is a widely held belief, as you've already seen, it's false.

Investors must pay annual fees for services from trust departments, investment counselors, and mutual funds. If they use brokers, the brokers will charge a commission for each transaction. If they use financial planners, they'll pay fees and/or sales loads on the various financial products offered by the planners. Anywhere investors turn there's a charge for advice and management unless they choose to do it themselves. What pro in his right mind would manage money for free?

When investors pay to have their money managed, they expect the professionals they're paying to earn their keep by studying the economy and stock market, by buying and selling when the time is right, and by going into cash in case the market should go down. Isn't that right? Would you pay an expert to spend little of his time taking care of your money? Of course not. You want that expert to be working—and working hard—on your behalf. You want that expert to spend as much time with your money as he can, and because you want that, he does what you expect.

Professionals rely heavily on forecasts of expected performance of the economy, the stock market, and individual companies. That's not too surprising because forecasting, especially of the economy, has been in existence for centuries. People from all walks of life are attracted to it. Everyone wants that special peek ahead. When Marco Polo returned to his homeland from the Orient, he told of kites used as economic-forecasting devices. Before a merchant ship embarked on a trading voyage, a drunkard (you had to be drunk to do this) was tied to a kite and launched from the ship's deck. If, and it was a big if, the drunkard actually made it into the air, the voyage was expected to be successful. But if he crashed, the trip was postponed if not canceled.

Despite the awesome academic evidence that forecasts are usually wrong (because no one can see into the future), many money managers continue to defy logic and rationality. It's not really mysterious, though, when you consider that millions of people still smoke and chew tobacco, despite the knowledge that tobacco is harmful; or continue to gamble at the racetrack, in lotteries or Las Vegas, although the house wins 99 percent of the time; or abuse drugs; or drive without seat belts fastened. Each money manager believes he has found the forecast (or forecasts) that will allow him to gaze profitably into the future, even though his counterparts won't be successful.

Let me take you on a brief journey through history to show you some of the most widely heralded predictions about the economy and stock market made by acclaimed experts:

1. Stocks have reached what looks like a permanently high plateau.

    —IRVING FISHER, PROFESSOR OF ECONOMICS AT YALE, OCTOBER 17, 1929

    Seven days later, on October 24, panic struck Wall Street and stock values plummeted.

2. The end of the decline of the Stock Market . . . will probably not be long, only a few more days at most.

    —IRVING FISHER TRYING TO REGAIN SOME OF HIS LOST LUSTER, NOVEMBER 14, 1929

    Nice try, Irving.

3. Financial storm definitely passed.

    —CABLEGRAM TO WINSTON CHURCHILL FROM BERNARD BARUCH, NOVEMBER 15, 1929

    Security prices had just begun their freefall into 1932.

4. Gentlemen, you have come sixty days too late. The Depression is over.

    —HERBERT HOOVER RESPONDING TO A DELEGATION RE- QUESTING A PUBLIC-WORKS PROGRAM TO HELP SPEED THE RECOVERY, JUNE 1930

What recovery? The economy hadn't come close to bottoming.

5. During the next four years . . . unless drastic steps are taken by Congress, the U.S. will have nearly 8,000,000 unemployed and will stand on the brink of a deep depression.

   —HENRY C. WALLACE, U.S. SECRETARY OF COMMERCE, NOVEMBER 1945

   Between 1945 and 1950, U.S. GNP rose nearly 50 percent.

6. Nineteen sixty promises to be the most prosperous [year] in our history.

   —ROBERT A. ANDERSON, U.S. SECRETARY OF THE TREA-SURY, APRIL 14, 1960

   Business conditions will stay good for some time to come. We are not about to enter any sharp recession.

   —HENRY C. ALEXANDER, CHAIRMAN OF THE MORGAN GUARANTY TRUST COMPANY, APRIL 22, 1960

   The recession of 1960 began that same month.

7. There ain't going to be no recession. I guarantee it.

   —PIERRE RINFRET, POPULAR ECONOMIST AND INVEST-MENT COUNSELOR, APRIL 1969

   The 1969–71 recession started the following summer.

8. There will be no recession in the United States of America.

—RICHARD NIXON, PRESIDENT, STATE OF THE UNION ADDRESS, 1974

The GNP dropped 5.8 percent the first quarter of 1974, and by July the economy was (you guessed it) in the deepest recession since the 1930s.

9. A drastic reduction in the deficit . . . will take place in the fiscal year '82.

—RONALD REAGAN, PRESIDENT, MARCH 1981

In fiscal 1982, the government had a record deficit up to that time—$110.7 billion.

Will Rogers once said, "An economist's guess is liable to be as good as anyone else's." In spring 1990, the National Association of Business Economists (whose main function seems to be polling itself) "guessed" that the remainder of the year and the several beyond it would be good. Specifically, 80 percent of the members predicted no recession for 1990, while 67 percent said there wouldn't be one of these nasty little events for at least three more years. In response to their poll, supercolumnist Alan Abelson of *Barron's* wrote, "Near-unanimity in this case breeds contempt. Anyone with even a taint of contrarian blood can only pray that, please, Lord, just this once, let 68 economists be right." Despite Abelson's plea, the economists were dead wrong. The deep recession of 1990–91 began shortly after the NABE poll was released.

The officials who decree the beginnings and endings of recessions pronounced that the last recession began in July 1990. Trouble was, they didn't announce this until April the following year. In December 1992, the same officials proclaimed the recession had ended in March 1991. The recession was already over before they knew it had started.

These are only a few examples of predictions that were way wide of the mark. I could provide hundreds of others, many of which in retrospect are quite humorous, but I think I've proved a point. David Dreman, author of *The New Contrarian Investment Strategy*, said, "Expert opinion—which investors naturally rely on—is very often wrong and not infrequently dramatically so." He devotes page after page to detailing the poor performance of the experts who try in vain to predict accurately.

If the evidence is so overwhelming that economic and stock-market forecasting is a fool's game, why do people rely on it so heavily? Eric Hoffer believed society is addicted to pollsters and forecasters. "Even when the forecasts prove wrong, we still go on asking for them. We watch our experts read the entrails of statistical tables and graphs the way the ancients watched the soothsayers read the entrails of a chicken."

The final word on why forecasting is so often awry comes from *The Futurist* magazine (January-February 1990):

Forecasts that a current trend will continue indefinitely are generally wrong, since most trends eventually reach a constraint.

Forecasts that describe ominous doom are frequently

wrong, since society usually addresses a problem once it has been identified as being critical.

Forecasts that describe a traditional solution to a critical problem are usually wrong. Society seems to find creative and innovative solutions.

The Futurist wasn't completely negative on forecasting. They believe forecasting can be much improved if it's based on analogy. The forecaster looks at past developments and sees how a similar sequence of events might happen in the future. That's the technique I've successfully used for years as an economic historian and superior stock picker.

Professional money managers try to make a perfect science of forecasting and investing. If they put A into a computer, they expect B to come out. Although B always follows A in the alphabet, it doesn't always follow A out of a computer. Thinking and acting this way creates frequent mistakes. No one knows where the Dow or the S & P 500 will be a year from now. No one knows how much money any company will earn in 1995. No one knows how strong the economy will be. Yet much of the typical professional's time is involved in trying to find the answers, all for nought.

Bennett W. Goodspeed, who in his own words "overcame the handicaps of having an MBA and working for several prominent Wall Street firms," wrote *The Tao Jones Averages: A Guide to Whole-Brained Investing* in 1983. It's a fascinating little book (154 pages). Goodspeed said analysts and portfolio managers "create an overload of information in their frenzied activity." I call it Paralysis from Overanalysis. Overload is harmful. In the words of the Chinese philosopher Lao-tzu, "The more stuffed the mind is with knowledge, the less able one can see what's in front of him."

Even if their forecasts for the economy and direction of the stock market were always on the money, most professional money managers would still rarely beat the market. The reason is the market has no operating expenses, but the professional does. Expenses eat sharply into returns.

Even to duplicate the market (not try to outperform it), the money manager has to trade frequently. Because stocks change multiple times in value every day, at any given time each stock in the Dow, the S & P 500, the Wilshire 5000, or any other market index he's trying to copy changes in its proportional weighting to all the others in the index. The cost of buying and selling to keep stocks in correct proportion (although that's not the only reason) almost singly guarantees that attempts to mimick the market will fail.

There are other excellent reasons why most professionals can't match the market. One is cash. Mutual funds have to keep cash available for their customers who wish to redeem shares. That amount usually ranges between 5 percent when they're optimistic on stock prices and 10 to 15 percent when they're negative. On any given day they must have a reserve in case more of their customers want to redeem shares than buy them. The fund manager doesn't want to be forced to sell part of his portfolio to pay for these redeemed shares. He always opts to dip into the cash reserve. For the long term, stocks earn three to four times as much as cash. The higher the fund's cash reserve, the more its return is penalized. Every fund has such a reserve, and every fund is damaged by it. The individual doesn't need a cash kitty, so his results aren't impacted.

Still another problem for money managers, including mutual funds, is forced panic selling. During the Great Crash of 1987, mutual funds were bombarded with so many redemptions they had to sell even though they may not have wanted to. Fortunately their phone lines were jammed with panicked callers. Otherwise they would have had to sell even more of their portfolios. This unplanned selling occurred, you guessed it, at or near the bottom. Once the chaos subsided, they had to reinvest at higher prices.

On Black Monday, October 19, I mailed a one-page memo to all my clients urging them to stand pat because there was blood in the streets, and you never sell when the blood is running. This is one Wall Street maxim that's true. I also told them to wait a few days for orderly trading to resume and then add to their portfolios. Those who heeded my advice not only recovered all their paper losses but also added greatly to their coffers. Mutual funds were forced to react. Savvy individuals responded and took advantage of what looked like a horrible situation but was in reality one of the premier buying opportunities in history.

When a financial institution (I include mutual funds) buys or sells shares of a company, it normally does so at various prices. Their buying and selling power is so enormous it affects their own transactions. Let's say you and a money manager hear on *Wall Street Week* a great idea that sparks new interest in an underfollowed New York Stock Exchange (NYSE) company that doesn't trade in big volume. The following Monday you call your broker to buy 100 shares, and the price is 28 (remember: stock prices don't need the dollar sign). For $2,800 plus commission you own the stock. At the same time, the money manager calls his broker and wants to buy 10,000 shares. He gets the first 2,000 at 28, the next 3,000 at 29, 3,000 more at $29\frac{1}{2}$, and the final 2,000 at 30.

Three years later the same analyst who recommended that stock is on *Wall Street Week* saying sell it. Coincidentally, you and the money manager are watching the show and both decide to sell on Monday. You call your broker and get out of your 100 shares at 42 less commission. The manager calls his broker and sells 3,000 at 42. Stock prices happen to be very weak that day, so the specialist handling the order on the NYSE takes the stock down a point on the next 3,000. Then he knocks it another $1\frac{1}{2}$ points and clears the remaining 4,000 shares.

In both of these situations, which aren't unusual, the fund's average cost to buy is higher than the individual's. The fund's proceeds from selling are lower. Financial institutions deal in thousands and tens of thousands of shares. Their buying and selling can drive stocks up or down before they complete their orders. It can take days if not weeks to accumulate or unload a position, whereas the individual can get in or out with one phone call with the price sometimes confirmed before he hangs up. This is another reason professionals have a tough time equaling or beating the market.

The Wall Street Journal asks, "How much does it really cost to have someone manage your money?

> Money managers and investment advisers all quote rates that seem straightforward enough. But the price that they give for their hand-holding usually doesn't include a variety of other charges investors typically end up paying. These include brokerage-firm trading costs to buy and sell stocks during the year and management and administra-

tion fees levied by mutual fund companies. There is also the cost of setting up a new portfolio in the first place.

The differences in total costs can be huge. Depending on the adviser's investment style, total annual costs can range from a low of about 1% of assets under management to 4%, or more. Initial costs of setting up a portfolio can run from less than 1% of the portfolio to 10% or more.

For the rest of this chapter, I'll stick solely to the costs involved with mutual funds, since this book is about creating your own mini-mutual fund and outpacing most existing funds. The first cost I'll discuss is the load. That's the charge you may incur to buy or redeem a fund's shares. No-load mutual funds don't charge anything, and they make up about half the equity funds.

The other half is load funds. Their loads go up to 8.5 percent, although that's extreme. The industry average is 3–4 percent. Most loads are front-end. They're deducted before you invest in the fund. A few funds have back-end loads that are taken out only when you redeem your shares. The top twenty-five general equity funds, led by Fidelity Magellan, have more than $210 billion under management. Fifteen have loads.

The services rating mutual-fund performance figure total returns—capital appreciation with dividends reinvested—but don't take loads into account. That makes comparing load funds to no-loads a more difficult chore, but there's one thing for certain. If a load fund and a no-load fund have exactly the same rates of return, the no-load will put more money into your pocket.

Taxes are another bugaboo. The performance-rating services usually don't consider them either. If your mutual funds are in a retirement account, they aren't a problem. But since the bulk of mutual funds is in taxable accounts, taxes are a sad reality. They can cripple returns, particularly if you're in a high tax bracket.

The Wall Street Journal wrote, "Beware Tax Consequences of Mutual Funds" in the February 22, 1992, edition. "Would you like to pay taxes on somebody else's gains? How about paying your taxes years earlier than you have to? Most people would answer both questions with a resounding 'No.' But mutual fund investors frequently subject themselves to such taxing situations, often without being aware of it." The *Journal* calculated how negatively taxes affected returns of the top ten mutual funds for the decade ending December 31, 1991.

Taxes took away one-quarter of the average total return during the ten years. That's a huge bite, a bite that could be completely eliminated if you assemble your own mini-mutual fund. As your own money manager, you control when to realize a capital gain; therefore, you control when to pay taxes on a gain. If you're in a mutual fund, that's a choice you don't have.

The National Bureau of Economic Research recently released its study "Ranking Mutual Funds on an After-Tax Basis" by economics professors Joel M. Dickson and John B. Shoven of Stanford University. Their study covered sixty-two growth and growth-and-income mutual funds with thirty-year records from 1963 to 1992 on a pretax and aftertax basis. One dollar invested in the Standard & Poor's 500 index in 1963 grew to $22.13 by the end of 1992. The median result for the sixty-two funds was that one dollar grew to $21.89 over the same period. Thus, the typical fund underperformed the stock market over the three decades, and that was before taxes. After taxes, the results were much worse.

For the thirty years, one dollar invested by an individual in a low-tax bracket grew to $16.45. The same dollar invested by someone in a medium-tax bracket grew to $12.82, while someone in the highest-tax bracket saw his dollar grow to just $9.87. Taxes took away 24.9 percent of the low-tax investor's return; 41.4 percent of the medium-tax investor's return; and a whopping 55 percent of the high-tax investor's return.

If taxes and loads aren't enough heavy yokes on the investor's shoulders, there are also annual administrative expenses and the management fee to consider. Mutual-fund administrative expenses range from $\frac{1}{2}$ percent to $1\frac{1}{2}$ percent of assets. Yearly management fees are in the same range. Together they cost the investor between 1 and 3 percent of total assets under management.

And finally there are trading costs. According to *Forbes* (November 23, 1992), "Turnover is, like the annual expense ratio, one of those numbers that fund vendors are compelled to disclose [in prospectuses] but that fund buyers all too often ignore. Just how great are transaction costs? Higher than you might think. A round-trip trade (a sell and a buy) executed on one of the stock exchanges probably costs a fund at least 0.35% of the transaction amount; for small, illiquid Nasdaq stocks the cost is closer to 1%. That's an annual cost of 1% to 3% for a fund reporting a 300% turnover." Even the best of funds have high turnover rates. That is, they literally sell and rebuy the equivalent value of the entire portfolio one or more times every year. Each time they buy and sell, two commissions—no matter how small—are paid. And those commissions eat into the investor's return.

With so many different costs associated with mutual funds, it gets confusing trying to see how they impact on returns. So I've put together a simple example that shows the hypothetical returns from Jazzy Fund versus Standard & Poor's 500 index for the next five years in a taxable account. You've already seen that most equity mutual funds can't equal the market (and that's before loads and taxes are considered), but to make this really interesting I've given the fund the return advantage. I assume Jazzy Fund will grow at 14 percent annually with the S & P 500 growing at 11 percent, one percentage point under its historic average.

Jazzy is a low-yield fund, so its return will be 2 percent from dividends and 12 percent from appreciation. S & P's total annual return will be 4 percent from dividends and 7 percent from appreciation, which is roughly the historic norm. One thousand dollars will be invested in the fund and the S & P index at the beginning of each of the five years. For ease of comparison, I assume no sales load to buy the fund nor any commissions to buy the S & P, and the investor in either is in the combined 35 percent tax bracket—28 percent federal and 7 percent state.

According to *Business Week* and a number of other reputable financial publications, mutual-fund returns in taxable accounts are 30–40 percent lower when both federal and state taxes are taken into account. Economists Shoven and Dickson said the take could be a lot more, so I'm being perhaps a little too biased in favor of mutual funds with this example.

At the beginning of year one, $1,000 goes into Jazzy.

During the year, $20 (2 percent) is paid out in dividends. After taxes at 35 percent, $13 is left. The fund rises 12 percent in value to $1,120 and like so many funds turns the portfolio exactly one time. This means the $120 gain is taxed at 35 percent, leaving a net gain of $78 for a total of $1,078. The fund charges a 1 percent management fee and another 1 percent for expenses. Those come out of the $1,078 leaving $1,056 after all expenses and taxes. Adding back in the $13 in dividends, $1,069 is left. That's a 6.9 percent net return.

One thousand dollars also goes into the S & P 500 at the beginning of the year. During the year the S & P pays $40 (4 percent) in dividends. After taxes $26 is left. The fund rises 7 percent in value to $1,070. There is no turnover, hence no capital gain, so the entire $1,070 is left. Add back in the $26 in dividends and the amount is $1,096, a 9.6 percent net return.

At the beginning of each of the next four years, $1,000 is added to both accounts. And the scenario above repeats each time. Please see the table on page 98.

Even though Jazzy Fund earns three percentage points more than the S & P every year, the S & P does better because there is no selling, hence no capital-gains taxes. If we continue the exercise, at the end of year ten the difference will be even more startling. Jazzy Fund will have grown to $17,134. The S & P will have swelled to $14,701.

Of course, you can argue this is an unfair comparison because the Jazzy Fund investor has already paid his taxes, and taxes are still owed by the investor who owns the "market." That's true to a degree but not as much as you may think. I have compared the S & P 500 index to a

	VALUE OF JAZZY FUND	VALUE OF S & P 500
End of Year 1	$1,069	$1,096
End of Year 2	2,212	2,297
End of Year 3	3,434	3,614
End of Year 4	4,740	5,056
End of Year 5	6,136	6,637

fund that outperforms it, a circumstance that doesn't happen too often.

Using America's Finest Companies, you're going to learn how to build your own mini-mutual fund that will consistently outdistance the market indexes. That's one reason capital-gains taxes won't be a hindrance. The other is almost all the mutual funds you'll compare your results to won't beat the indexes as in the example above. They'll be behind.

Benjamin Graham was right when he said the individual has many advantages over the financial institutions. One major advantage is that you, the individual, can control your own financial destiny rather than be at the mercy of someone else. The other major advantage is that you can assemble your own equity mini-mutual fund, equal or beat the market year in and year out, and outperform 75 percent of the investment professionals. Then, it won't be just the stockbrokers and other investment pros who can afford to buy yachts. You'll be able to afford one, too.

CHAPTER SIX

Let Uncle Sam Help You Get Where You Want to Go

The reward of energy, enterprise and thrift—is taxes.

—WILLIAM FEATHER

For most families, the two most important financial goals are educating children and having enough money to live comfortably in retirement. I prefer to call it life after work because retiring has connotations of being old and inactive, when the opposite is usually true. If a man or woman reaches age sixty to sixty-five in good health, odds are very high he or she will live at least another twenty years.

One of the biggest problems older people in this country face is living a long, healthy life but not having enough money to travel and do whatever else they wish in their later years.

The typical married couple reaching age sixty-five has about $7,000 in liquid assets in addition to Social Security benefits and possible home ownership. At the rate you're spending money today, how long would $7,000 last? Two months? Three months? Four months? I doubt it would be beyond four months if that long.

Having enough money for life after work is easily achievable when you start early enough and invest your money on a regular basis. If you've already started, that's great. If not, it's still not too late, and you have lots of company. *Money* magazine conducted a survey a few years ago and discovered one of four people between ages forty-five and sixty-five has set aside nothing for life after work. Three out of four said they hadn't saved enough to live in the style they desired, and nearly one of two said their biggest fear was not having enough money to carry them through life after work. Those that were preparing for life after work said their preferred investment was a savings account, which historically has not kept up with inflation and taxes. Just 25 percent bought shares of stock, the best inflation hedge of all.

It's easy to see why so many people aren't prepared for life after work. If you're in your twenties or thirties, you're still some thirty to forty years away. Even if you're in your mid-forties as I am, it will still be about two decades before you reach sixty-five. Somehow twenty, thirty, or forty years seems so far away we imagine there's still plenty of time to get ready for life after work, so why worry about it now? That's the way all those who haven't begun planning think. If they don't think that way, then why haven't they started?

Another reason people don't get ready for life after work is they don't save any money. All their income is spent to pay the grocer, the mortgage company, the auto dealer, the department store, the phone company, the local utility, the doctor, the TV repairman, the movie theater, the video-rental store. The list goes on and on. These people spend every dollar they make. Sometimes they spend more than they make and borrow to make up the difference. They reason that one day they'll start to save some money as soon as they quit spending so much. But few really ever do it. It's a fantasy.

To be able to invest, you've got to be able to save. The first place you ought to invest your savings is in a retirement plan. The only way you'll be able to invest in a retirement plan is to budget for it using my formula:

Bill Staton's Only Investing Formula

---

100 percent of your income
− contribution to your retirement plan
− all other expenses

= 0

The formula far too many individuals are using is, unfortunately, not the one above but the one below. Although they haven't written this formula down, in their minds they've budgeted all their money for everyone else and nothing for themselves. That's why they reach life after work in a near-bankruptcy state.

100 percent of your income
− 100 percent for expenses
_____

= 0 for your retirement plan

Before spending all your income, first allocate a certain percentage for investment. The amount can be 1 percent of pretax income, 2 percent, 5 percent, 10 percent, or more. It's up to you. You need to start with some percentage, even if it seems tiny, and then gradually increase it as you can. Logically, the higher your level of income, the higher the percentage taken out. Andrew Carnegie, the steel magnate, said, "You want to know if you will be rich? The answer is, 'Can you save money?'"

Because I see so many adults failing to prepare for their financial futures, I have a strong sense of mission about teaching young people how to manage their money so they'll end up where they want to be financially. I know the earlier they start the easier it will be and the more likely they are to make it. Why? Because saving and investing are a habit, one of the best habits there is. Once a person adopts the saving-investing habit, it's as hard to quit as smoking.

Each year I have the privilege of teaching Junior Achievement's superb applied economics course to juniors and seniors at my daughter's school. I always spend a lot of time on investing because that's the subject I know the most about. I've just completed my fifth year, and I think I learn more than the students do. These eager juniors and seniors tell me they "waste" between $10 and $15 per week. This is money that slips through their hands. They don't know where it goes. They just know it disappears.

The lesson I try to get across is that if they invest that "wasted" money in a retirement plan at 12 percent per year, the rate of return from stocks since World War II, they'll end up with $1 million or more. Even minors can have retirement plans, as I'll show later. And yes, it is possible to invest in a well-diversified portfolio of stocks with that small amount of money. I'll demonstrate how easy it is. You don't have to go the customary mutual-fund route and end up with inferior results.

By simply beginning at sixteen to invest $50 per month at 12 percent in an individual retirement account (IRA)— and never increasing the amount—a 16-year-old will have $1,749,977 by the age of 65. If he waits until 18, the amount will be $1,377,071. By waiting two more years until age 20, he will have only $1,083,462. That's still more than a million dollars, but it's $666,515 less than the one who started at 16. The sixteen-year-old, who makes 48 more payments of $50 per month (a total of $2,400 extra) than the 20-year-old, will wind up with 62 percent more money at age 65. Clearly, the earlier you start investing, the more money you'll have when you need it.

A few years ago Theodore Johnson died in Delray Beach, Florida, at age ninety. Mr. Johnson never made more than $14,000 a year, working for United Parcel Service, but he invested a dollar or two in UPS stock every chance he got. When he retired in 1952 his stock was worth $700,000. When he died it had mushroomed to $70 million, and he left more than half of it to help disadvantaged young people get educations. If a man who never made more than $14,000 in a single year can become a multimillionaire, so can you.

Two young people aged nineteen graduate from high

school. Both begin to work and have annual incomes. Investor Smart (a graduate of one of my Junior Achievement classes) opens an IRA through a stockbroker and begins to salt away the annual maximum of $2,000. He makes his contributions at the beginning of each year. Investor Not As Smart (who wasn't in my class) decides to wait a few years to open his IRA.

Investor Smart contributes $2,000 annually from age 19 through age 26 and quits. After contributing a total of $16,000, he decides (wrongly, in my opinion) to make no more contributions until he begins to withdraw funds from his IRA at age 65.

Investor Not As Smart, at age 27, wakes up to the realization he needs to begin preparing for retirement. He opens an IRA through his stockbroker and contributes $2,000 per year from age 27 through age 65, all the while earning 12 percent (the stock market's historic return) annually on his money as does Investor Smart.

For brevity, I've not shown every year, but Investor Not As Smart contributes $78,000 over the thirty-nine years he contributes to his plan. Thus, he puts nearly five times more into his IRA than Investor Smart. But when both are sixty-five, Investor Smart has $818,786 more than Investor Not As Smart. Even if Investor Not As Smart continues to invest $2,000 per year forever, he will never catch up with Investor Smart, who committed just $16,000. This is the best example I know to demonstrate the power of investing early for a new home, vacation, college education, life after work, or whatever.

Life after work will require a lot more money for some than for others. What will it take for you? When I launched my financial coaching career, the accepted rule of thumb was that if you were living comfortably on what you made when you were close to retiring, it would cost about 60 percent of that amount once you quit work. The theory sounded plausible. Your children were grown and gone. Since you were in your sixties, you weren't as active as when you worked. You didn't eat out as frequently, didn't travel as often, didn't buy as many "things" as before, etc. I guess the "experts" who came up with the 60 percent figure assumed everyone who retired sat around and played cards, or if they were really active played rousing games of shuffleboard in between naps.

Today we know the truth. More and more older people are very active and mentally alert. George Burns, Milton Berle, Bob Hope, and my great aunts, Dot and Gladys, immediately come to mind. Burns is approaching a hundred, with Hope and Berle trailing not too far behind. I'm reminded of George Burns's quick response to the question "What's the secret of your longevity?" He responded, "I look forward to getting out of bed each day."

I'm also reminded of what Eubie Blake, the famous jazz pianist, said on his hundredth birthday: "If I'd known I was going to live this long, I'd have taken better care of myself." He died at 104. Dot and Gladys have taken excellent care of themselves. Gladys is the oldest of eleven children and is now 92. Baby sister Dot is only 90. They both spend much of their summers at Maple Grove, our 112-year-old family home in Hendersonville, North Carolina. Although they do require some help, especially Gladys, both these joyful ladies basically do for themselves. They didn't slow down a bit even at age 80. They zoomed through it like it wasn't there.

The most recent studies indicate people spend between

AGE	Investor Smart		Investor Not As Smart	
	IRA CONTRIBUTION	YEAR-END VALUE	IRA CONTRIBUTION	YEAR-END VALUE
19	$2,000	$ 2,240	0	0
20	2,000	4,748	0	0
21	2,000	7,559	0	0
22	2,000	10,706	0	0
23	2,000	14,230	0	0
24	2,000	18,178	0	0
25	2,000	22,599	0	0
26	2,000	27,551	0	0
27	0	30,857	$2,000	$ 2,240
28	0	34,560	2,000	4,748
29	0	38,707	2,000	7,559
30	0	43,352	2,000	10,706
35	0	76,401	2,000	33,097
40	0	134,645	2,000	72,559
45	0	237,290	2,000	142,105
50	0	418,186	2,000	264,668
55	0	736,987	2,000	480,665

60	0	1,298,823	2,000	861,327
65	0	2,288,969	2,000	1,532,183
Less Total Invested		(16,000)		(78,000)
Net Earnings		**$2,272,969**		**$1,454,183**
Money Grew (at 12%)		**143-fold**		**20-fold**

80 and 90 percent of their final working year's income in the first few years of life after work. The erroneous 60 percent figure of yesteryear wasn't in, or even close to, the ballpark. These same studies also show people emphatically do not want to reduce their lifestyles unless they're forced to.

If a young person begins his or her career around age 25, he or she will work for the next 35 to 40 years. During that period, money will have to be set aside for the 20 to 30 years of life beyond work. Social Security won't support more than a meager lifestyle at best. Fewer and fewer companies have pension plans employees don't have to contribute to. The chance of winning the lottery is one in many millions. Providing for the future is up to each individual, or else the future won't be provided for short of a substantial inheritance appearing out of the blue.

To calculate approximately how much you'll need in the future is easy. Just fill in the worksheet on page 109. You can use it over and over as your financial needs change.

For someone my age to be making $50,000 a year is not unreasonable, nor is it an outrageous amount of money. Fifty thousand dollars doesn't go nearly as far as it used to. I want to enter a comfortable life after work at age 65, which is only 19 years away. Inflation is a factor of life, and I want to take that into account. For this illustration, I assume it will increase at 4 percent per year in the future. That's higher than the rate for the last 70 years but about in line with the past 20. The higher the inflation number I plug in, the more conservative my estimate will be. Using the Rule of 72 (the inflation rate × the rate of return = 72), I divide the inflation rate, 4, into 72 and ar-

HOW MUCH DOES LIFE AFTER WORK COST?

The pretax income I need in 1995 to live
comfortably is $\underline{\$50,000}$ (A)

My current age is $\underline{46}$ (B)

The number of years until I begin life
after work is $\underline{19}$ (C)

I think inflation will average __4__% (D) each year
until I retire. My cost of living will double every
__18__ (E) years [E = 72 divided by D and rounded].

My cost of living will double __1.06__ (F) times
between 1995 and the year I retire. [F is
calculated by dividing E into C.]

My income the first year of life after
work will need to be
G = [1 + F] × A × 90%. $\underline{\$92,700}$ (G)

My income __18__ (E) years after I begin
life after work will need to be 2G.
[2G = H] $\underline{\$185,400}$ (H)

---

rive at 18. At a 4 percent inflation rate, the cost of living
doubles roughly every eighteen years. If I use 3 percent,
the number of years is 24; at 5 percent it's 14½.

If I'm doing well on $50,000 in 1995 and have nineteen
years until life after work, my cost of living will increase
1.06 times. I multiply $50,000 times 2.06 and find that in
2014 what costs $50,000 today will cost a little more than

twice as much—$103,000. My first year of life after work (when I'm sixty-five) I'll be spending at 90 percent of that rate, which is $92,700. Longevity runs in my genes, so I will probably live another eighteen years beyond that, at which time I'll be eighty-three. With inflation staying at 4 percent, my cost of living will double to $185,400, and since I fully expect to make it to three digits, I'll make it another eighteen years beyond that. My cost of living in the year 2050: $370,800. And don't forget, that's an annual, not a lump sum, number. It will take nearly $400,000 each year to live comfortably.

With a 4 percent inflation rate, the cost of living will slightly more than double every two decades. How many decades have you got to live? Once you make a stab at that figure, it's easy to zero in on how much the next twenty, thirty, forty, fifty, sixty, or more years will cost.

Life after work will take a lot more money than most people think, especially given they don't like to reduce their lifestyles and will probably live longer than expected. Wouldn't it be terrible to have plenty of good years left and a zest for life but no money for anything more than the bare necessities?

The simplest way to invest for life after work is to participate in your company's contributory 401(k) retirement plan or its equivalent, the 403(b), if you work for a government agency or nonprofit institution. Under the typical 401(k) arrangement, you can contribute up to 15 percent of your pretax income or $9,240 in 1994 (this amount is adjusted upward for inflation each year), whichever is lower, and invest your money in a variety of mutual funds. Few 401(k)s allow you to invest in individual stocks other than the stock of the company offering the plan.

Your choices usually range from three to about fifteen different mutual funds, plus one other—a GIC, guaranteed investment contract.

With a 401(k) or any other retirement plan to which you make annual contributions, the amount is excluded from your gross income for federal and state income tax purposes. Let's say you earn $50,000 pretax in 1995 and invest $4,000 in your company's 401(k). Your reported gross income will be reduced to $46,000. The taxes you would have paid on the $4,000 in your 401(k) are now invested for your future. This is how Uncle Sam becomes your partner when you invest in a retirement plan. He doesn't tax you on the dollars you put into it. Neither does the state where you live. Those unpaid tax dollars work for you tax-free until you begin withdrawals (which are then taxed many years down the road).

Uncle Sam will help you another way, too. He has made it expensive to voluntarily enter your retirement plan. Short of a loan, financial hardship, and a few other special considerations, once you invest money in any retirement plan you're not allowed to get it out before age $59\frac{1}{2}$ without a 10 percent penalty on the amount removed. Plus you'll have to pay taxes, too. Yes, you can move your retirement funds from one plan to another. But you cannot spend the money unless you want to pay a high price. Because Uncle Sam doesn't want you to squander your retirement funds, he becomes an excellent financial friend.

Since you're probably not going to be able to structure your own portfolio of America's Finest Companies in your 401(k), let me offer some advice to help you make the most of your investment dollars. First, put every single dollar you can into a 401(k). Besides the initial tax deduction, your money grows free of taxes until you begin taking it out. This is reason enough to participate, but there's another goody that lots of 401(k) participants can enjoy— a matching contribution from their employer.

The average company chips in fifty to sixty cents for every dollar the employee sets aside, sometimes up to 6 percent of pay. In the example above, the employee earning $50,000 puts $4,000 into his 401(k) in 1995. That's 8 percent of pretax income. His employer puts in fifty cents for every dollar up to 6 percent of pretax income. Six percent is $3,000. The company adds $1,500, so the total contribution for 1995 is $5,500. Even before the employee's money is invested, he's already made a 37.5 percent return on his money ($1,500 divided by $4,000). Where else can anyone get such a phenomenal return on his money with absolutely no risk? The employer is actually paying employees to invest, and they're saving taxes to boot.

Assuming our theoretical employee is forty, sets aside $4,000 per year (with a $1,500 company match) through age sixty-five, and the money grows at 12 percent in stock funds, he'll be worth $821,337. Without the $1,500 match, his money will grow to $597,336. The employer match is worth an additional $224,000. The match adds firepower to a 401(k). It's the equivalent of adding a rocket engine to a race car.

It seems a no-brainer to invest in a 401(k) and it is, but about 40 percent of Americans who can participate don't invest anything. Sadly, they'll live to regret it. Of the 60 percent who do participate, most don't invest as much as they should and could. And most invest too conservatively. They opt for money-market funds, so-called low-risk bond funds, and GICs, which guarantee a fixed return. These alternatives barely keep ahead of inflation. Too few people have their money in stock funds, which are the only places to maximize their returns. A 1993 survey of more than two hundred California companies revealed two-thirds of 401(k) assets were in GICs and money-market funds. Stock funds were avoided because they are misperceived to be too risky.

According to a *Wall Street Journal* survey, only 8 percent of all U.S. companies with one hundred and fewer employees have retirement plans. This means more than 30 million Americans will not have retirement plans unless they set them up for themselves. If you're one of the 30 million, pay close attention. I'm going to give an overview of the most common retirement plans that are simple and inexpensive for you to set up. This isn't an exhaustive treatment of the subject. Too many other books have already done that. There are dozens at your local library with lengthy sections on the various retirement plans, and quite a few are dedicated exclusively to the subject. There's more available on retirement plans than you want to know or need to know.

The IRA—individual retirement account—has been available to just about everyone since 1982. Any individual, including a minor, with earned income from salary, commissions, or bonuses (interest and dividend income don't count) can set aside up to $2,000 each year in an IRA. The amount goes up to $2,250 for a married couple with one person working outside the home.

Until Congress passed tax "reform" legislation in 1986, any amount invested in an IRA was deductible from gross income. For example, if a twenty-one-year-old in college earned $3,500 from odd jobs, the student could put as much as $2,000 of that into an IRA. Only $1,500 would be taxable. Today, money going into an IRA may be totally tax deductible, partially tax deductible, or not deductible at all. If you aren't covered by a pension plan, you can deduct every dime that goes into your IRA.

If you're married and one of you is covered by a company retirement plan, the contribution is fully deductible only if annual adjusted gross income is $40,000 or less. Singles covered by a retirement plan at work may deduct the full IRA amount if they earn $25,000 or under. Couples earning between $40,000 and $50,000 and singles earning between $25,000 and $35,000 can deduct part of their IRA contributions. Above $50,000 and $35,000 gross income, respectively, there's no deduction. But gross income can be reduced. Here's how.

Let's suppose a super-saving young couple has an adjusted gross income of $50,000 annually before plan contributions. Each has a 401(k) and participates to the limit, and each can save an additional $2,000 to go into an IRA. As a couple, they set aside the maximum 15 percent—$7,500—into their 401(k)s. After the 401(k) contributions, their adjusted gross income is cut to $42,500. For each of the $2,000 IRA contributions, $1,500 is deductible. The other $500 isn't.

To avoid confusion, the man and woman set up two IRAs apiece—one for money that is tax deductible; the other for money that isn't. When money begins to be withdrawn from the IRAs, which can be as early as age $59\frac{1}{2}$ with no penalty imposed by the IRS, all the money from the tax-deductible IRA is taxed at the individual's rate in the year it's taken out. With a nondeductible IRA, taxes are paid on only part of the money withdrawn under an IRS formula.

If your situation doesn't allow you to deduct any of your IRA contributions but you can still afford to kick in $2,000 a year, I suggest doing it. The benefit to you is all the money grows with no taxes as long as the money remains in the account.

An IRA can be established at almost any financial institution—bank, savings and loan, credit union, stock brokerage. There may be a modest setup charge and what's called an annual maintenance fee in the $50–$100 range, although some firms waive all fees if the account is large enough. Discount broker Charles Schwab charges nothing for retirement accounts with at least $10,000 of assets. Since you're going to be buying shares of America's Finest Companies in your IRA, you want what's called a self-directed account. This means you call the shots and decide what to buy and sell.

For the self-employed like me, there are two other retirement accounts to know about. In a sense, they are gigantic IRAs because they share many of the same features yet allow investors to sock away far more than $2,000 annually. The first is a SEP—simplified employee pension—which is almost identical to an IRA, with one huge difference. You can contribute 15 percent of your self-employment income up to a total of $30,000 per year.

As with an IRA, you can establish and contribute to a SEP for the present year as late as when you file taxes in the following year, including extensions. I don't recommend waiting that late. The earlier you make your annual contribution to a retirement plan, the harder the money will work for you. I'll show you what I mean. You have a

SEP for twenty-five years and salt away $5,000 per year, which earns 13 percent in a portfolio of America's Finest Companies. In the first instance, you invest the $5,000 on the first business day of the year. In the second, you invest the $5,000 the last business day of the year. By investing on the first day of the year instead of the last, you'll wind up with $879,250 rather than $778,098. That's a $101,152 increment on the same investment of $125,000 over two and a half decades. Quite a difference, isn't it?

SEPs can be opened at the same places as IRAs. So can another type of retirement plan, the Keogh. Like the SEP, a Keogh can be used if you're full-time or part-time self-employed. If you're eligible, you can contribute up to 20 percent of pretax income each year or $30,000, whichever is lower. Keoghs offer more flexibility than SEPs, and there's more paperwork involved, too. Another difference is a Keogh has to be set up by December 31 of the year in which you make the first contribution. As with a SEP, you can wait until tax-filing time to make the contribution.

Keoghs come in several types. One is the money-purchase Keogh, which allows up to 20 percent of annual self-employment income (with a $30,000 ceiling) to go into the plan. The hitch is that once you start you must put in the same percentage of income every year unless there's a loss. Skipping a contribution or falling short of the stated percentage may subject you to a huge tax penalty.

Another Keogh is the profit-sharing variety. The beauty of this plan is you can make or not make a contribution each year. You still have the $30,000 upper limit, but the percentage is lower—13 percent.

A defined-benefit Keogh allows you to put away as

much as 100 percent of your self-employment income to guarantee a certain minimum annual withdrawal once you retire. The nearer you are to life after work, the more income you can defer each year. A tax expert or actuary will need to help you if this is the route you choose to go. With the defined-benefit Keogh, you may be able to quickly "catch up" with where you need to be if you haven't planned for retirement and are in your late forties or fifties.

SEPs and Keoghs can be used for small businesses with more than one employee, and there are other retirement plans that might fit your particular needs. I won't get into them here, but I will reiterate the advantages of all contributory retirement plans. One, the money added each year reduces your gross income, hence your current tax liability. Two, your money grows with no tax consequences until it's taken out. Three, the federal government frowns on early withdrawals, so it pays you to stick with your plan. Four, you have the tremendous opportunity to create your own mini-mutual fund of America's Finest Companies within your retirement plan. By doing that, your money will grow steadily at an above-average rate.

CHAPTER SEVEN

Be Your Own Money Manager

Everyone has a scheme for getting rich that will not work.

—MURPHY, ORIGINATOR OF MURPHY'S LAW

One nice thing about being your own money manager and investing exclusively in America's Finest Companies is you'll only have to spend an hour or two each year (the equivalent of a long lunch) on your investment portfolio or portfolios. Then you're finished for another 365 days. It will be that easy and take that little time. This is the message I spread wherever I give a keynote address or lead a workshop. I continually butt heads against the skeptics (mostly professionals who fail to match the market indexes) who say investing can't be that easy, otherwise everyone would be doing it. But it is.

If you'll follow the steps outlined in this chapter, you can ignore daily or weekly gyrations in stock prices. In fact, you can forget about what the Dow Jones industrials, the S & P 500, or other market indexes are doing. Wouldn't that be a big relief? You can also safely ignore all forecasts about the direction of the economy and interest rates. Which way they head won't matter to you.

For the moment picture yourself as the biblical character Noah. God told you the worst storm ever was going to occur in a few months, and you needed to build a boat to withstand the coming forty-day flood. How would you have prepared for such an unprecedented event?

Noah knew. He built the craft to strict proportions to withstand the most horrible storm in history. Replicas have been tested in laboratories under hurricane conditions. Even in storms of that magnitude, the ark remained upright at all times. It never came close to capsizing.

The same principles Noah used to construct his ark are the principles you can use to guide your portfolio through economic and stock-market storms of the future. Whatever happens, you will survive and prosper because you'll know what to do, and what not to do. Your success will not be tied to how much time and effort you spend keeping up with the economy, interest rates, and the anticipated direction of stock prices.

If you love reading about business and investing, you'll probably want to continue subscribing to the publications that deal with these subjects. I suspect, though, you're heavily involved—as a parent, in your business or profession, as a community volunteer. You have little time to track stocks actively or follow the economy, and you don't want to either.

What you'll learn in this chapter will allow you to feel good about everything you're not reading. If you spend a lot of money on newspapers, magazines, and newsletters you don't want to read, cancel them. You can save hundreds of dollars every year, and the savings can go into your portfolio.

Step No. 1. Be Patient

My philosophy of investing is anchored in patience. George F. Baker, founder of First National Bank of New York, the forerunner of Citicorp, said patience is one of three prerequisites for making a fortune in stocks. He knew time is on the side of the investor. He also knew that the longer anyone invests, the better his results will be. History proves it.

Since stock trading began in America in the late 1700s, the longer-term trend has been relentlessly upward. Even the Great Depression of the 1930s appears to be nothing but a blip on a two-hundred-year chart of stock prices. Naturally there are frequent, wide, day-to-day, month-to-month, and even year-to-year swings. But given enough time, stocks go only one way—UP!

Benjamin Franklin counseled, "He that can have patience can have what he will." This advice is certainly on the money for stock investors. It happens to be right for investors in every other field, too. If you'll be patient and give your stock investments time to work for you, you'll be uncommonly successful. Time (as opposed to timing) is on the side of the investor.

Perhaps the most patient investor in the world, and without question the most successful, is Warren Buffett, chairman of Berkshire-Hathaway on the New York Stock Exchange. Buffett was one of Benjamin Graham's students at Columbia University. He learned his lessons well. Berkshire-Hathaway is the most expensive stock in America and has traded for more than $17,000 per share. Buffett is one of America's wealthiest people with an estimated net worth in excess of $8 billion.

Warren Buffett is frequently quoted in the financial media because he has tremendous insight coupled with a quick wit. Many of his quotes are among my favorites, but perhaps the most useful for you is his response to the question "How long should you hold a stock?" Buffett has often said, "Our favorite holding period is forever." Talk about patient. What could be more patient than holding a stock forever?

I'm not asking you to hold any stock forever, but I am asking you to buy and hold for perhaps many years. I want you to be a long-term buyer and owner of America's Finest Companies and sell only when necessary, which won't be that often. You may go for years at a time without selling shares of any company you own, but all the while you'll be buying. Think of a young child. Children are natural accumulators. They want to be surrounded with things—dolls, stuffed animals, toys, books, games—and they rarely want to get rid of any of them. When you invest, I want you to be like a child.

What I recommend is easy. Pick your portfolio of at least five companies, each in a different industry, from the listing in the appendix. Invest the same dollar amount in each. Once a year when the new-edition list comes out from the author, see if the stocks you bought the previous year are still included. If they are, buy more. If one happens to have been dropped, sell and replace it with another one of America's Finest Companies.

Step No. 2. Buy More of What You Already Own

When you buy more of what you already own each year, you'll be employing the time-proven way to buy shares of the Finest Companies at reasonable prices. This technique is one you'll seldom read about in investment books. It's the only way I know to make money in any stock environment, including the Great Depression. It demands 100 percent commitment to building a diversified portfolio of quality companies. What's the way? It's dollar-cost averaging—buying the same dollar amount of common stocks over time, i.e., quarterly, semiannually or annually. I prefer once a year because that's easy to remember and requires less record keeping.

Under dollar-cost averaging, there is absolutely no need to predict the short-term direction of stock prices. We already know the long-term direction is up. If you continue buying stocks through good and bad years, dollar-cost averaging keeps the average cost of your purchases below their average market price, guaranteeing you a profit. Here's why.

If you buy a portfolio of stocks today and their prices fall every year for the next three years (as in the Great Depression), each time you buy additional shares you'll purchase them at a lower price than before. Each time you buy more, you'll lower the average cost per share until the stocks bottom and begin to go up again. Think of buying a $400 suit. It goes on sale three months later for $300, so you buy another one in a different color because the price is so attractive. Your average cost per suit drops from $400 to $350. If you buy a third suit for $200, you'll drive the average cost down again to $300. Each suit is still worth $400, but the average cost per suit is $100 less than that.

Assuming the companies you invest in are chosen from the America's Finest universe, their stock prices will stop falling at some point and then resume their long-term uptrends. Once those uptrends begin, you'll discover your average cost per share is under the market value. You'll have a profit. On the other hand, if your stock portfolio

A SIMPLE EXAMPLE OF DOLLAR-COST AVERAGING

STOCK PRICE	QUARTERLY INVESTMENT	SHARES PURCHASED	CUMULATIVE AVERAGE COST PER SHARE
10	$1,000	100.0	$10.00
9	1,000	111.1	9.47
8	1,000	125.0	8.93
7	1,000	142.9	8.35
6	1,000	166.7	7.74
5	1,000	200.0	7.09
6	1,000	166.7	6.91
7	1,000	142.9	6.92
8	1,000	125.0	7.03
9	1,000	111.1	7.19
10	1,000	100.0	7.38
Total	$11,000	1,491.4	

goes up immediately and continues up, you'll have a profit, too. Either way, you'll make money. That's the extraordinary attraction of dollar-cost averaging using America's Finest Companies.

Under dollar-cost averaging, it's a mathematical certainty you'll always make money as long as the companies you buy don't go out of business. If you stick exclusively with America's Finest Companies, you won't have to worry about that. A company headed for serious trouble will be delisted well before it gets there.

Assume you invest $1,000 at the beginning of 1995 in an America's Finest Company that doesn't pay a dividend. The cost is 10 (note: stock prices are written without the dollar sign) per share. You purchase 100 shares. One quarter later the stock has fallen to 9, and you spend another $1,000. The price is 10 percent lower than when you began. Instead of purchasing 100 shares, you get to buy 111.1 shares. The next quarter the price falls to 8. Then to 7, 6, and 5 in subsequent quarters. Every three months you buy $1,000 of stock.

After six installments you've invested $6,000 of your hard-earned money. The stock has collapsed 50 percent in price. Even though you are very discouraged, you continue to add to your holdings because the company is sound. You believe the stock will eventually come back.

The stock finally turns around and slowly climbs to 7. At this point, the average cost of all shares purchased is $6.92. You have a small profit. From here the profits grow larger as the stock rebounds toward the original price at which you first purchased it.

Eventually the stock recovers to 10. By now you have

invested $11,000 total. The stock, first purchased for 10 per share, is still only 10. It had zero appreciation. That's the bad news.

The good news is you paid an average $7.38 for each share purchased. Your profit is $2.62 per share (excluding dividends, which would boost profits if included). The shares are valued at $14,914, a handsome return of 35.6 percent in 2½ years. And the stock is no higher than when you started.

Dollar-cost averaging worked great for an investor even during the most hostile stock-market environment in American history—the Great Depression. Nineteen twenty-nine had to be the worst time ever to start an investment program. How did dollar-cost averaging leave you if you'd been unfortunate enough to begin investing, even in the soundest of companies, on the eve of the Great Depression?

Assume you invested $1,000 on December 31, 1929. Stocks prices had already crashed and begun to come down. The worst was yet to come. Standard & Poor's 500 index was 21.4. With $1,000 you would have bought 46.6 "shares" of the index. These shares produced $46 in annual dividends, which were set aside until December 31 the following year. By then the S & P had fallen 28.5 percent to 15.3. You acquired 68.2 more shares for $1,046 (your $1,000 plus the $46 in dividends).

The next December you invested another $1,000, plus $94 in dividends, and bought 134.7 shares of the S & P 500. It plunged 47.1 percent in 1931 for a dreadful 62.2 percent cumulative loss since you started just two years earlier. Time really flies when you seem to be losing

YEAR END	REINVESTED DIVIDENDS	ANNUAL AMT. INVESTED	CUMULATIVE TOTAL INVESTED	S & P 500 12/31	TOTAL SHARES	MARKET VALUE	ANNUAL DIVIDENDS
1929	—	$1,000	$1,000	21.4	46.6	$1,000	$46
1930	$46	1,046	2,046	15.3	114.8	1,761	94
1931	94	1,094	3,140	8.1	249.5	2,026	125
1932	125	1,125	4,265	6.9	412.8	2,844	182
1933	182	1,182	5,446	10.1	529.8	5,351	238
1934	238	1,238	6,685	9.5	660.1	6,271	310
1935	310	1,310	7,995	13.4	757.7	10,176	546
1936	546	1,546	9,540	17.2	847.7	14,563	678

money as fast as hackers lose golf balls. At the end of 1932, the market was down a whopping 67.8 percent. You had shelled out $4,265. Your portfolio was worth $2,844, a dismal 33.3 percent loss, but only half the S & P's loss.

Because you knew dollar-cost averaging demanded total devotion (at this point it seemed more like total insanity), you continued to plunk down $1,000, plus dividends, at the end of each year. By December 31, 1935, you'd invested a total of $7,995. Your gain was 27.3 percent while the S & P index was down 37.4 percent from the end of 1929. One year later you'd made a 52.7 percent profit ($14,563 divided by $9,540) while the index was still almost 20 percent under water.

Dollar-cost averaging is mechanical and overcomes one of the investor's worst enemies, his emotions. Emotions encourage people to buy stocks at exorbitant highs and to dump them at ruinous lows. Dollar-cost averaging puts emotion on the back burner where it belongs and gives every investor the opportunity to amass the shares of highest-quality companies—America's Finest—at reasonable (and sometimes bargain) prices. Dollar-cost averaging unfailingly produces superior results even if you have the misfortune always to buy at market peaks.

T. Rowe Price, a large mutual-fund company, proved that the commitment to invest is far more important than timing the investment. Said another way, "time in" the market is much more valuable than "timing" the market. Their study calculated the growth of a $2,000 annual IRA contribution invested in "shares" of Standard & Poor's 500 index at its highest level each year from 1969 through 1988. On July 31, 1989, the account was worth $171,757, more than four times the total investment of $40,000 spread over two decades. The compound annual total return was 10.1 percent. At that rate, money doubles every seven years, quadruples in fourteen, and expands eightfold in twenty-one.

AMCAP, a mutual fund, came up with similar results in its study covering 1973–92. A $5,000 investment at each year's market peak had grown to $460,356 by the end of 1992. In their example, 1974 and 1975 were the only two years in which the investor would have been under water.

Even if you wanted to, you couldn't invest at the highest point for stock prices every year for twenty straight years. You probably couldn't do it once. But even if you did, your results would still be excellent—and better than from any other investment. With America's Finest Companies, they'd be exceptional.

Step No. 3. Diversify Your Holdings

How many stocks do you need in your portfolio? You can start with one, but I recommend saving enough money until you can purchase five, each in a different industry. Then you can work your way toward seven, eight, or ten, perhaps even to twelve. More than that is excessive. Warren Buffett's Berkshire-Hathaway has major stakes (more than $400 million) in fewer than ten companies, and remember that he's worth more than $8 billion. At the end of 1992, his company's four largest holdings were $1.5 billion of Capital Cities ABC (which used to be in America's Finest Companies but had a down-earnings year in 1991 after twenty up years in a row), $3.9 billion of Coca-Cola,

	NUMBER OF STOCKS	REDUCTION IN RISK AS % OF POTENTIAL
Underdiversified	2	46.3%
	4	72.0
Well-Diversified	6	81.0
	8	85.7
	10	88.5
Overdiversified	20	94.2
	50	97.7
	100	98.8

$2.2 billion of GEICO, and $1.4 billion of Gillette, all of which are AFC companies. A number of studies show you can achieve about 90 percent of the benefits of diversification with as few as seven to eight companies, as long as each is in a different industry.

This diversification table was adapted from Richard A. Brealey's excellent book *An Introduction to Risk and Return from Common Stocks* (Cambridge, Mass., and London: The M.I.T. Press, 1969). Others will be somewhat different, but all reach the same conclusion.

A ten-stock portfolio provides 88.5 percent of the possible advantages of diversification. Five stocks provide 77.4 percent, twenty stocks 94.2 percent. Once you own eight to ten stocks, each in a different industry, adding others reduces risk almost imperceptibly. It's hardly worth the time and effort to own lots of stocks. Warren Buffett has proved it.

Step No. 4. Buy Only the Shares of America's Finest Companies

There's no special skill to making above-average profits in stocks if you (1) are patient and have an investment horizon of at least five to ten years, (2) add to your holdings regularly, (3) diversify properly, and (4) invest only in the shares of companies that will remain in business and have rising earnings and dividends. Virtually anyone, even a young person, can name at least twenty or thirty companies that fit this mold.

When my daughter was ten she picked a market-beating portfolio of eight stocks without my help. In the spring of 1988, about six months after the biggest stock crash in history, I wanted her to learn a little something about investing her own funds. She had slightly more than $4,000 cash in her college fund; the remainder was already invested.

I asked Gracie, as I fondly call her, to pick eight companies she'd like to own and purchase $500 of each through our stockbroker. It took her only a few minutes to come up with eight names. One was a private company that makes stuffed animals. Another was a yogurt chain, which neither of us knew much about. She scotched those two names and came up with two more. One was Pizza Hut, which is owned by PepsiCo. So she bought PepsiCo. She loves Coca-Cola, too, and bought $500 of that. She also loves Jeep, which is owned by Chrysler.

She was using the copier at my office, so Xerox was one stock to buy. Gracie reasoned electricity and phones will always be in vogue. She purchased Duke Power and BellSouth. She also added McDonald's and NCNB (now NationsBank, headquartered here in Charlotte).

That's a great portfolio, don't you agree? It's high quality and well diversified, even though Coca-Cola and PepsiCo are in the same business. All eight companies are likely to survive the worst downturn in the economy any of us can imagine. How do I know that? Because all but one, McDonald's, survived the Great Depression. Even though America's Finest Companies wasn't in existence at the time, five of the eight are in it—Coca-Cola, Duke Power, McDonald's, NationsBank, and PepsiCo. Even a ten-year-old knew that you should always buy the finest companies.

How has the portfolio done? Gracie bought her stocks on May 2, 1988. Through the end of the first quarter of 1994, the Dow Jones industrial average gained 80.7 percent, excluding dividends. Her group of eight stocks appreciated a whopping 131 percent and beat about two-thirds of all professionals.

There are several ways to pick a portfolio from America's Finest Companies. The technique you use is not nearly as important as that you invest in nothing but the companies listed. If a company's not in America's Finest Companies, why own it? America's Finest Companies have at least ten years in a row of higher earnings or dividends per share. Seventy-three qualify on both counts. Only 3 percent of all U.S. public companies make the cut. They have the most consistent growth records. That's why they're going to make money for you regardless of how you pick the portfolio. You can bank on it because the track record is so good. Here's a list of the top performers for the past decade through December 31, 1993.

For the ten years through December 31, 1993, AFC companies gained 324 percent in price (excluding divi-

COMPANY	PRICE CHANGE
Franklin Resources	6873%
Biomet	1618
Tootsie Roll Industries	1474
William Wrigley Jr.	1461
Clayton Homes	1406
Crompton & Knowles	1347
Cooper Tire & Rubber	1147
Progressive Corp.	1007
Circuit City Stores	971
Newell Co.	957
A. Schulman Inc.	953
Wal-Mart Stores	946
State Street Boston	924
Telephone & Data Systems	899
Coca-Cola	898
Century Telephone	888
Hasbro Inc.	883
Crown Cork & Seal	872
Gillette	871
PepsiCo	856
Cintas Corporation	854
Nordson Corporation	849
Stryker Corporation	812
Bemis	793
Heilig-Meyers	790

dends) compared with 182 percent for the S & P 500. That's 78 percent better than the market. During the same period, 308 (74 percent) at least doubled in price; 196 (47 percent) at least tripled. As important, only a handful declined.

Most people will fill their portfolios with companies they've heard of. You probably will, too, and that's an excellent way to assemble your portfolio. Scan the alphabetical list of names in the appendix and circle or check the ones you like. If you need an eight-stock portfolio, you can probably find eight companies you like that are in different industries, before you get into the Ds.

If you feel you need a certain amount of dividend income, your search may be limited to all the stocks yielding 4 percent and more. There are 122 of those. If you'd rather go for companies that pay little or nothing, you might choose from among the stocks yielding 1 percent or less. There are 43 of those. Maybe you like certain industries, such as banking, utilities, or consumer products. Instead of searching for companies by name, you'll scan the list in the appendix and pay close attention to the industry categories.

Another method to build your portfolio is to choose stocks randomly but not by throwing darts or drawing names. For example, you need eight stocks. Start anywhere on the list and pick every twentieth or thirtieth company until you have eight in various industries. Or pick one company from the As, Cs, Es, Gs, Is, Ks, Ms, and Os or any other group of eight letters you like. It really doesn't matter so much how you pick because you'll end up with a great portfolio in any case.

Step No. 5. Maintain the Same Dollar Amount in Each Stock

When you've chosen your portfolio of at least five companies, the next thing is to purchase approximately the same dollar amount of each. (We'll get into how to open an account and deal with a broker in Chapter 10.) The first place to establish your portfolio is a retirement plan, since money will grow without tax consequences until withdrawn. For now, assume your retirement account is already open. If you're buying five companies, put 20 percent of your money into each. With eight companies, $12\frac{1}{2}$ percent in each; with ten, 10 percent in each. Don't make the mistake so many professionals make when they try to apportion their money among the "best" companies and industries. That's speculation.

For example, a portfolio manager believes drug/health care stocks are undervalued, so he puts 25 percent of his funds into that sector. He also thinks utilities won't do nearly as well, so only 5 percent of his money goes there. When you allocate, you introduce guesswork into what otherwise is a simple process of spreading your money equally among all your holdings. Anyone can speculate about which groups and individual companies have the most promising outlooks, but that's about all they can say. They can't be sure they're going to be right until after the fact. You and I already know we can't peek into the future. I still don't understand why so many professionals believe they can.

Once you've purchased your portfolio, what's next? Nothing. You don't have to do anything until a year has passed. Let dividends accumulate in your account or automatically reinvest them (see Chapter 8). On the first anniversary date of your initial purchases, put more money into your account and buy more of what you already own.

Here's an example of what to do. With $5,000 cash in your IRA, you decide to buy $1,000 of each of five companies. You'll add a sixth later. To make this example easier, I won't take commissions into account in the initial purchases. To make it more convincing, I'm using five of America's Finest Companies, each in a different industry, and going back to the first business day of 1988, January 2, so I can use real results.

The five companies I chose would all have been in America's Finest Companies on that date and still are. They are American Brands, a consumer-products company; Aon Corporation in insurance; Bristol-Myers Squibb, a major pharmaceutical firm; Emerson Electric, a capital-goods company; and SCANA, an electric utility.

I purposely chose five stocks that as a group appreciated far less than the market over the past five years. The odds anyone could pick five underperformers are about two out of a hundred. Odds are only one out of a hundred of choosing six. Even with this handicap, I'll demonstrate the awesome power of dollar-cost averaging and reinvesting your dividends.

It's important for you to know that I did not know in advance how this exercise was going to turn out, nor did I know what the results would be from year to year. I went through it as if I were in your shoes.

During the next twelve months, the market value of your portfolio rises 15.2 percent in value, from $5,000 to $5,760. Four stocks move higher in price, with American Brands the biggest gainer. Emerson Electric drops in price and becomes the most underweighted. At the end of 1988, here's the value of each stock ranked in descending order of value. Note each company raised its dividend during the year (a trait of America's Finest Companies), so total income is higher by 9.0 percent at year's end than at the beginning.

It's time to add another $2,000 annual contribution to

JANUARY 2, 1988

COMPANY/DIVIDEND	SHARE PRICE	NUMBER SHARES	COST	ANNUAL INCOME
American Brands/$1.16	22	45	$990	$52.20
Aon Corp./$1.26	23	43	989	54.18
Bristol-Myers Squibb/$1.68	41	25	1,025	42.00
Emerson Electric/$1.03	35	29	1,015	29.87
SCANA/$2.38	28	35	980	83.30
		Total	$4,999	$261.55
		Money uninvested	$ 1	

DECEMBER 31, 1988

COMPANY/DIVIDEND	SHARE PRICE	NUMBER SHARES	VALUE	ANNUAL INCOME
American Brands/$1.26	32	45	$1,440	$56.70
Aon Corp./$1.37	28	43	1,204	58.91
Bristol-Myers Squibb/$2.00	45	25	1,125	50.00
SCANA/$2.45	32	35	1,120	85.75
Emerson Electric/$1.16	30	29	870	33.64
			$5,759	
		Money uninvested	$ 1	
		Total	$5,760	$285.00

your IRA. That, coupled with the $261.55 in dividends collected in the account in the first year, plus the $1 uninvested, is $2,262.55 ($2,263 rounded) for investment. Adding $2,263 to $5,760 ($8,023) and dividing by five means there should theoretically be $1,604 in each stock (again ignoring commissions). In theory, you'd buy $164 more American Brands, $400 more Aon, $479 more Bristol-Myers Squibb, $484 additional SCANA, and $734 Emerson Electric. That sounds fine on paper, but in reality it's impractical because there are commissions to consider. Most brokers charge a minimum $30 to $40 per transaction. At those rates, between $150 and $200 of the $2,263 new money to invest would be eaten up by commissions. That's too much, so I suggest a different tack.

With the $2,263, buy more of the two companies that are the most underweighted. If you used my full-service broker, you could buy thirty-five shares of SCANA for $1,120 plus roughly $40 commission ($1,160) and thirty-five Emerson Electric for $1,050 plus approximately $40 commission ($1,090). (All commissions are estimates.) There'd be $13 left in the account. The account would then look like this, with SCANA and Emerson Electric clearly overweighted, at least for now.

By the end of the second year, all five stocks have moved higher. Total value of the portfolio is $9,810, a 23.5 percent increase from the beginning of the year. Here's where the portfolio stands, with highest value at the top (following page).

Since it's the beginning of year three, it's time to kick another $2,000 into your IRA and redeploy that amount, plus the $411.35 in dividends and the $13 left over from the previous year. The total market value of your stocks is

JANUARY 2, 1989

COMPANY/DIVIDEND	SHARE PRICE	NUMBER SHARES	MARKET VALUE	ANNUAL INCOME
SCANA/$2.45	32	70	$2,240	$171.50
Emerson Electric/$1.16	30	64	1,920	74.24
American Brands/$1.26	32	45	1,440	56.70
Aon Corp./$1.37	28	43	1,204	58.91
Bristol-Myers Squibb/$2.00	45	25	1,125	50.00
			$7,929	
Money uninvested			$ 13	
Total			$7,942	$411.35

DECEMBER 31, 1989

COMPANY/DIVIDEND	SHARE PRICE	NUMBER SHARES	MARKET VALUE	ANNUAL INCOME
SCANA/$2.51	36	70	$2,520	$175.70
Emerson Electric/ $1.28	39	64	2,496	81.92
Aon Corp./$1.49	42	43	1,806	64.07
American Brands/ $1.41	35	45	1,575	63.45
Bristol-Myers Squibb/$2.12	56	25	1,400	53.00
			$9,797	
Money uninvested			$ 13	
Total			$9,810	$438.14

$9,797. That, together with the $2,424 to reinvest, adds up to $12,228, or $2,447 per stock. SCANA and Emerson Electric are a little above that. Leave them alone. The other three are less than their proportionate weighting, with Bristol-Myers Squibb most underrepresented, followed by American Brands.

What you want to do is take the $2,424 you're adding to your portfolio and buy more shares of American Brands and Bristol-Myers Squibb. Buy twenty-one more shares of Bristol-Myers Squibb for $1,176, plus $40 commission ($1,216), and thirty-three of American Brands for $1,155 and a $40 commission ($1,195). There's $13 left over. Now the portfolio looks like this:

JANUARY 2, 1990

COMPANY/DIVIDEND	SHARE PRICE	NUMBER SHARES	MARKET VALUE	ANNUAL INCOME
American Brands/ $1.41	35	78	$ 2,730	$109.98
Bristol-Myers Squibb/ $2.12	56	46	2,576	97.52
SCANA/$2.51	36	70	2,520	175.70
Emerson Electric/ $1.28	39	64	2,496	81.92
Aon Corp./$1.49	42	43	1,806	64.07
			$12,128	
		Money uninvested	$ 13	
		Total	$12,141	$529.19

The portfolio has a modest gain in 1990 of 3.2 percent, but as in every year since the portfolio was begun, each of the five companies again raises its dividend. Your portfolio is now worth $12,610 with annual dividend income of $570.90, more than twice as much as when you started.

DECEMBER 31, 1990

COMPANY/DIVIDEND	SHARE PRICE	NUMBER SHARES	MARKET VALUE	ANNUAL INCOME
American Brands/$1.60	41	78	$ 3,198	$124.80
Bristol-Myers Squibb/ $2.40	67	46	3,082	110.40
Emerson Electric/$1.34	38	64	2,432	85.76
SCANA/$2.60	34	70	2,380	182.00
Aon Corp./$1.58	35	43	1,505	67.94
			$12,597	
	Money uninvested		$ 13	
		Total	$12,610	$570.90

At the beginning of year four, you're going to invest another $2,000 along with the $529.19 in dividends collected during the previous year and the $13 of uninvested funds, a total of $2,542. That figure added to the portfolio's $12,610 brings the total to $15,152. This means that ideally $3,030 should be invested per stock.

A quick glance at the portfolio shows American Brands and Bristol-Myers Squibb to be slightly overweighted. Emerson Electric and SCANA aren't too far off the mark, while Aon is about half what it should be. Aon needs $1,525 more to bring it up to its ideal average. The portfolio is also big enough now to add a sixth company, which is what I would suggest.

Let's assume you pick Wallace Computer Services as your sixth company. You buy forty shares of Aon for $1,400 and $40 commission ($1,440). That leaves just $1,102 to go into Wallace. You buy fifty-three shares at

20, plus $40 commission. There's just $2 left. This is the portfolio at the beginning of the fourth year.

JANUARY 2, 1991

COMPANY/DIVIDEND	SHARE PRICE	NUMBER SHARES	MARKET VALUE	ANNUAL INCOME
American Brands/$1.60	41	78	$ 3,198	$124.80
Bristol-Myers Squibb/$2.40	67	46	3,082	110.40
Emerson Electric/$1.34	38	64	2,432	85.76
SCANA/$2.60	34	70	2,380	182.00
Aon Corp./$1.58	35	83	2,905	131.14
Wallace Computer/$0.51	20	53	1,060	27.03
			$15,057	
	Money uninvested		$ 2	
	Total		$15,059	$661.13

Your fourth year investing is very satisfying as your portfolio tacks on 24.0 percent more value. Again, as in every previous year, each of your companies raises the dividend. Now it's time to make another $2,000 contribution, alongside $661 of dividends and $2 of uninvested funds—$2,663. The portfolio is worth $18,669, so $3,555 should be apportioned to each of the six holdings ($21,330 divided by six). Bristol-Myers Squibb has the largest weighting. Emerson Electric is second and is just a few dollars off its ideal. Aon, SCANA, and American Brands aren't too wide of the mark either. Wallace Computer Services is $2,283 less than it should be.

Rather than make this complicated and to save commis-

DECEMBER 31, 1991

COMPANY/DIVIDEND	SHARE PRICE	NUMBER SHARES	MARKET VALUE	ANNUAL INCOME
Bristol-Myers Squibb/$2.76	88	46	$ 4,048	$126.96
Emerson Electric/$1.40	55	64	3,520	89.60
American Brands/$1.81	45	78	3,510	141.18
Aon Corp./$1.66	39	83	3,237	137.78
SCANA/$2.67	44	70	3,080	186.90
Wallace Computer/$0.55	24	53	1,272	29.15
			$18,667	
Money uninvested			$ 2	
Total			$18,669	$711.57

JANUARY 2, 1992

COMPANY/DIVIDEND	SHARE PRICE	NUMBER SHARES	MARKET VALUE	ANNUAL INCOME
Bristol-Myers Squibb/$2.76	88	46	$ 4,048	$126.96
Wallace Computer/$0.55	24	161	3,864	88.55
Emerson Electric/$1.40	55	64	3,520	89.60
American Brands/$1.81	45	78	3,510	141.18
Aon Corp./$1.66	39	83	3,237	137.78
SCANA/$2.67	44	70	3,080	186.90
			$21,259	
Money uninvested			$ 11	
Total			$21,270	$770.97

sions, too, I'd invest the whole $2,663 in Wallace. Buy
108 shares at 24. Assuming $60 in commissions, the total
spent is $2,652 with $11 remaining. How will this work
out? Let's go to the end of 1992 and see.

Nineteen ninety-two wasn't a great year, since your

DECEMBER 31, 1992

COMPANY/DIVIDEND	SHARE PRICE	NUMBER SHARES	MARKET VALUE	ANNUAL INCOME
Aon Corp./ $1.77	54	83	$ 4,482	$146.91
Wallace Computer/$0.60	27	161	4,347	96.60
Emerson Electric/$1.47	55	64	3,520	94.08
American Brands/$1.97	40	78	3,120	153.66
Bristol-Myers Squibb/$2.88	67	46	3,082	132.48
SCANA/$2.73	40	70	2,800	191.10
			$21,351	
	Money uninvested		$ 11	
		Total	$21,362	$814.83

portfolio increased less than 1 percent. Nonetheless, it was up. Wallace Computer Services and Aon Corporation scored nice gains. Emerson Electric was flat while Bristol-Myers Squibb lost 21 points, American Brands shed 5 points, and SCANA fell 4.

To date, you've shown the following results and a profit every year for five straight years:

1988	+15.2%
1989	+23.5
1990	+ 3.9
1991	+24.0
1992	+ 0.5

This is equivalent to a compound annual return of 13.0 percent, one percentage point better than the market's return since World War II. And remember, it was achieved with six stocks that all lagged the market, in some cases by a wide margin.

At this point you have a portfolio that's grown from $5,000 at the beginning of year one (1988) to $21,362 at the end of five years (1992). You added $2,000 per year for four years, which combined with the original capital of $5,000 is a total of $9,000 invested. The $12,362 difference (137 percent more than you put in) is from appreciation and dividends reinvested. Annual dividend income is now more than three times what it was just five years ago.

The portfolio is out of balance because Aon and Wallace Computer Services are far larger than the other four positions. You're going to add another $2,000 at the start of 1993, and along with that $771 in dividends and the $11 uninvested. That adds up to $2,782 new dollars to invest. By adding $2,782 to the portfolio's value, $21,362, we get $24,144, which works out to $4,024 per stock. You could purchase thirty-five shares of SCANA for $1,390 and $40 commission ($1,430), and nineteen Bristol-Myers Squibb for $1,273 plus $40 commission ($1,313). There'd be $29 left over.

JANUARY 2, 1993

COMPANY/DIVIDEND	SHARE PRICE	NUMBER SHARES	MARKET VALUE	ANNUAL INCOME
Aon Corp./$1.77	54	83	$4,482	$146.91
Bristol-Myers Squibb/$2.88	67	65	4,355	187.20
Wallace Computer/$0.60	27	161	4,347	96.60
SCANA/$2.73	40	105	4,200	286.65
Emerson Electric/$1.47	55	64	3,520	94.08
American Brands/$1.97	40	78	3,120	153.66
			$24,024	
	Money uninvested		$ 29	
	Total		$24,053	$965.10

DECEMBER 31, 1993

COMPANY/DIVIDEND	SHARE PRICE	NUMBER SHARES	MARKET VALUE	ANNUAL INCOME
Wallace Computer/$0.64	34	161	$5,474	$103.04
SCANA/$2.74	50	105	5,250	287.70
Aon Corp./$1.80	48	83	3,984	149.40
Emerson Electric/$1.56	60	64	3,840	99.84
American Brands/$1.97	33	78	2,574	153.66
Bristol-Myers Squibb/$2.92	58	65	3,770	189.80
			$24,892	
	Money uninvested		$ 29	
		Total	$24,921	$983.80

At the beginning of 1994, you make the regular $2,000 contribution to your portfolio, which was up again for the sixth year in a row. That, coupled with $965 in dividends accumulated in 1993 and the $29 uninvested funds in your

JANUARY 2, 1994

COMPANY/DIVIDEND	SHARE PRICE	NUMBER SHARES	MARKET VALUE	ANNUAL INCOME
Wallace Computer/$0.64	34	161	$5,474	$103.04
SCANA/$2.82	50	105	5,250	296.10
Bristol-Myers Squibb/$2.92	58	85	4,930	248.20
American Brands/$1.97	33	130	4,290	256.10
Aon Corp./$1.80	48	83	3,984	149.40
Emerson Electric/$1.56	60	64	3,840	99.84
			$27,768	
	Money uninvested		$ 28	
		Total	$27,796	$1,152.68

account, adds up to $2,994. Add that figure to the $24,921 portfolio value and you have $27,915—$4,653 ideally invested in each of the six companies.

The two smallest positions are Bristol-Myers Squibb and American Brands. You can buy more of each: fifty-two shares of American Brands ($1,716 and $50 commission) and twenty Bristol-Myers Squibb ($1,160 and $40 commission), a total investment of $2,966. There's $28 uninvested.

Now wait to see your results in 1994 and then rebalance the portfolio again.

Although there's no practical way to keep exactly one-sixth of your portfolio in each of the six companies, you've done an excellent job so far by buying more shares each year of the one or two most underweighted companies in the portfolio. You're getting more than 80 percent of the benefits of diversification with just six companies. With occasional juggling, you can keep the portfolio in good proportion while still adding the annual $2,000 maximum and reinvesting all dividends. The balance doesn't have to be perfect, only as exact as you can make it.

STEP NO. 6. SELL RARELY

To recap: Start with a portfolio of at least five of America's Finest Companies. Each year check the latest compilation of America's Finest Companies to see whether all the companies you own are still included. If they are, buy more as shown above. If one's been knocked out of the box, replace it with another. By using this simple approach, you'll sell infrequently while simultaneously con-

tinuing to accumulate shares of the finest companies on the market.

Stock-market and investing books are chock-full of all sorts of information, much of it half-baked, about how to time the market and sell at the right times. I'm not very good at selling because it's much more difficult to know when a stock is overpriced than it is to know when it's underpriced. Spotting a cheap stock and buying it is easy for me. Finding one that's not going any higher and may be headed for a fall is a lot tougher.

That's why I recommend only three reasons to sell. One is to bring a stock that's overweighted in your portfolio back into line. You sell part of it. Two is to get rid of a stock that's been dropped from America's Finest Companies. You sell all of it. Three is you need the money. You may sell part or all of your holdings depending on how much money is required. Other than these, I recommend buying and not selling.

I'm in the camp with Warren Buffett. Buffett says he loves buying, but selling is a different story. He compares the pace of his selling activity with a traveler stranded in Podunk's lone hotel. There was no TV in the room, so the stranger faced a long unfruitful evening. However, he soon discovered a book on his night table called *Things to Do in Podunk*. Excitedly opening it, the traveler found only a single line, "You're doing it."

You can be your own successful money manager by following these six steps:

1. Be patient.
2. Buy more of what you already own.
3. Diversify your holdings.

4. Buy only the shares of America's Finest Companies.

5. Maintain the same dollar amount in each stock.

6. Sell rarely.

Of course you can make managing your money a lot more complicated than this. Most professionals and ordinary folk do. But it's not necessary. Why make money the hard way if there's an easier way? That's what I've always asked myself. By the time I was thirty-one, I had earned my first million from investing in stocks. I spent a lot of time analyzing and agonizing over my portfolios. Within five years, I was worth more than three million. Getting to that point was a lot easier because I was simplifying the process. Today my personal investment process is the same one I'm advocating for you. It's easy to understand, simple to put into practice, and most important, it works.

How do commissions eat into returns? In my example, you started with $5,000 and added $2,000 at the start of each of the next six years. My best guesstimate is commissions would eat a maximum 5 percent of the $2,000 annual contribution, leaving $1,900 to actually go to work for you. If your portfolio just matched the historic 12 percent return from stocks since World War II, you'd have $46,972 at the end of ten years. The initial $5,000 would earn 12 percent for the entire period. That would be worth $15,529. You'd make nine annual contributions of $1,900, which would also grow at 12 percent. They'd make up the difference of $31,443.

People who don't believe in using anything other than mutual funds are going to leap all over my example. They'll say it's outrageous for you to pay as much as 5 percent a year in commissions on a $2,000 investment. In a no-load mutual fund, the entire $2,000 (rather than $1,900) would go to work for you. That's correct to a point. But don't forget there are ongoing management and operating expenses for *all* mutual funds, which typically are at least 2 percent and may be as much as 4 percent each year. If mutual funds charged nothing, proponents would have a stronger case.

Opponents of my method will also mention this or that mutual fund that has, according to some mutual-fund survey, beat the pants off the market in recent years. They'll wonder why you weren't investing in those funds. Good question. In Chapter 5 I proved most funds fail even to equal the market every year, let alone beat it. The percentage of stock funds that will beat the market over any ten-year period is remarkably small—less than 5 percent from 1983 to 1993. Will you be able to pick the market beaters from more than one thousand funds? I'll give odds you won't, and I'll win more than enough bets to retire wealthy from the bets alone.

America's Finest Companies, as a group, have consistently beaten the market by several percentage points, either from capital appreciation alone or with dividends reinvested. The eleven stocks from the Super 50 Team with dividend reinvestment plans returned 22.9 percent compounded annually versus 16.2 percent from the S & P 500. That's a 6.7 percent difference. Suppose five of those stocks were your portfolio over the past decade and commissions were a whopping 10 percent on each $2,000 investment as well as on the initial $5,000. The first $4,500 ($5,000 less $500 commission) investment would have grown to $35,377. The remaining nine $1,800 annual contributions ($2,000 less $200 commission) would have piled up to $52,135, a total of $87,512. That same money invested in the market, assuming no loads or annual fees, would have amounted to $63,503 or $24,009 less.

GETTING STARTED WITH A LITTLE OR A LOT

I've showed you how to start with $5,000 and add $2,000 a year, the maximum allowed by law, to an IRA. But you may have a lot less than that to begin with, or you may have a lot more.

Suppose you're eighteen and in college. You get a job as I did when I was in school and earn $2,500 each of the four years you're there. You need most of that money for living expenses but can invest $50 each month. Since you have earned income, you're allowed to contribute to an IRA.

You open an account with a discount brokerage firm (where commissions are cheaper) and mail them a $50 check monthly for twelve months; this is invested in a money-market fund earning 3 percent. At the end of the year you've saved $600 and earned about $9 interest. Pick one stock you like from America's Finest Companies and buy it. Less $35 estimated commission (because you're using a discount broker) you'll put roughly $574 to work. Follow this same routine each of the next three years you're in school and buy a different stock each time. Make sure it's in a different industry.

When you graduate, you'll have invested $2,400 (less commissions) and will own a few shares of four different companies. Since you're armed with a college degree, you should soon start earning far more than $2,500 and be able to contribute the maximum $2,000 per year if your employer doesn't offer a 401(k) plan. If your employer does, you should invest in his plan first because you can salt away far more than $2,000 a year. For this example, I'm assuming you're not covered at work.

You're now twenty-two and your little IRA has grown to $4,000. No doubt it's out of balance. When you make your first $2,000 annual contribution, you'll have enough money to add a fifth stock in a different industry. Follow the same technique outlined earlier to invest $2,000 annually and maintain balance. Sounds simple, and it is.

Now let's shift gears for a minute and pretend you're self-employed. No one else works with you. You realize you've got zero dollars set aside for life after work and need help, so you rush out and purchase a copy of this book. After completing Chapter 6 on retirement plans, you open a SEP or Keogh. Take your pick. You fund it with a $10,000 contribution at age 50 and bump up the contribution each year by 10 percent. By age 60, you're up to $25,937 annually, which is $4,063 less than the maximum $30,000 you're allowed to contribute under today's law. By the time you're 60 the limit is probably going to be significantly higher. Your money grows at 12 percent each year, the same rate as common stocks since World War II. Since you're investing exclusively in America's Finest Companies, it ought to grow at 13–15 percent, but I'm being conservative.

You see from this example that after eleven annual contributions (at the beginning of each year), you've put $185,310 into your SEP or Keogh. When you are age 65,

A SEP/KEOGH GROWS RAPIDLY EVEN WHEN YOU START LATE

START AGE	ANNUAL $ CONTRIBUTION INCREASES 10% ANNUALLY/EARNS 12% TAX DEFERRED	
50		10,000
51		11,000
52		12,100
53		13,310
54		14,641
55		16,105
56		17,716
57		19,487
58		21,436
59		23,579
60		25,937
Total Contributions:	$185,310	
Worth at Age 65:	$551,112	
Worth at Age 70:	$971,248	
Worth at Age 75:	$1,711,671	

it will have grown to $551,112 (nearly tripled) and five years later will be approaching a million dollars (more than quintupled).

If you can start a portfolio with as much as $10,000 and add at a rate similar to this, you should spread the money equally among six companies rather than five. In the illustration you could stay with six stocks until age 55 and then add a seventh, which ought to be sufficient diversification. Again, you'll follow the same technique described earlier.

CHAPTER EIGHT

The Awesome Power of Reinvested Dividends

Whenever you see the compound annual returns from the Dow Jones industrial average and Standard & Poor's 500 composite index, they include quarterly reinvestment of all dividends. Without dividend reinvestment, annual returns from stocks would be about as exciting as watching a silent movie.

One dollar invested in the S & P 500 at the end of 1925, with dividends reinvested, mushroomed to $727.38 by the end of 1992. John Connallon, an investment strategist at Smith Barney, asked a number of the firm's research analysts to guess what percentage of the $727.38 was from capital appreciation and what was from dividend reinvestment. The average guess came in at 60 percent capital gains, 40 percent dividend reinvestment. The answer is that $693.22 or 95.3 percent was from reinvested dividends while 4.7 percent ($34.16) was from capital gains. Said another way, dividends reinvested generated more than twenty times the return from capital appreciation.

Approximately one thousand companies allow you to automatically reinvest your dividends in shares of their stock through DRPs—dividend reinvestment plans. Two hundred ninety-one of America's Finest Companies (71 percent) have them; twenty-seven offer a discount to market price in addition. The standard way to open a DRP is to buy a few shares of a company (like Hershey Foods) that offers it and have the shares registered in your name. The shares are then mailed directly to you, along with a simple DRP signup form. You fill in a few blanks and return it to the company. Each quarter instead of mailing you a dividend check, Hershey and every company in whose DRP you participate will send you a form like the one shown on the following page.

All DRP statements are similar and easy to read. This one is the statement of my five-year-old son, Will, who owns more than four hundred shares of this particular company. He also participates in four other DRPs. You probably already guessed the companies are among America's Finest. Since he's a minor, an adult has to be custodian of the account. In this case Will's mother is his custodian.

The bottom left-hand corner of this statement shows that 412 shares are owned by Will and registered in his name outside the plan. Just to the right of that number,

DIVIDEND REINVESTMENT AND
STOCK PURCHASE PLAN

Public Service Company
Of North Carolina, Inc.

SHAREHOLDER
ACCOUNT NUMBER:
XXXX
TAXPAYER IDENTIFICATION
NUMBER

FOR SHAREHOLDERS OF PUBLIC SERVICE COMPANY OF NORTH CAROLINA, INC.   **XXX-XX-XXXX**

ADDRESS ALL CORRESPONDENCE TO:
FIRST UNION NATIONAL BANK, AGENT
DIVIDEND REINVESTMENT SERVICE
TWO FIRST UNION CENTER
CHARLOTTE, N.C. 28288-1154
(1-800-829-8432)

JOHN DOE
1111 MAIN STREET
CHARLOTTE NC 11111

AMOUNT ENCLOSED:

_____

TO MAKE AN OPTIONAL CASH PAYMENT, PLEASE DETACH AND MAIL WITH YOUR CHECK

FOR SHAREHOLDERS OF PUBLIC SERVICE COMPANY OF NORTH CAROLINA, INC.

Shareholder Account Number:	Taxpayer Identification Number	Investment Date	Record Date	Dividend Payment Date	Quarterly Dividend Rate Per Share
XXXXX	XXX-XX-XXXX	10/01/93	09/10/93	10/01/93	$.19750

DATE OF TRANSACTION	TYPE OF TRANSACTION	AMOUNT OF TRANSACTION	SERVICE CHARGE	NET AMOUNT INVESTED	PRICE PER SHARE	SHARES ACQUIRED OR WITHDRAWN	TOTAL SHARES HELD IN PLAN
					PRIOR BALANCE ◆◆◆◆◆◆ ➤		10.1880
01/04/93	STOCK DIVIDEND	0.00	.00	0.00	0.0000	5.0940	15.2820
04/01/93	COMMON DIVIDEND	78.28	.00	78.28	16.2450	4.8187	20.1007
04/01/93	PLAN DIVIDEND	2.90	.00	2.90	16.2450	0.1785	20.2792
07/01/93	COMMON DIVIDEND	81.37	.00	81.37	15.6988	5.1832	25.4624
07/01/93	PLAN DIVIDEND	4.01	.00	4.01	15.6988	0.2554	25.7178
10/01/93	COMMON DIVIDEND	81.37	.00	81.37	17.5038	4.6487	30.3665
10/01/93	PLAN DIVIDEND	5.08	.00	5.08	17.5038	0.2902	30.6567

PLAN DATA FOR CURRENT PERIOD

FIVE-DAY AVERAGE CLOSING PRICE	PURCHASE PRICE		AVERAGE OR HIGH AND LOW PRICE ON	
	WITH REINVESTED DIVIDENDS	WITH OPTIONAL CASH PAYMENTS		
18.425	17.5038	18.425	10/01/93 17.875	

Shares held on record date				TOTAL DIVIDENDS PAID	TAX WITHHELD IF ANY	NET DIVIDEND REINVESTED	SERVICE CHARGES	SHARES ACQUIRED WITH REINVESTED DIVIDENDS AND OPTIONAL CASH	TAXABLE DIVIDEND INCOME
HELD BY YOU	HELD IN PLAN								
FULL	FULL	Fraction							
412	25.7178		Current	86.45	0.00	86.45	0.00	4.9389	88.29
			Year to Date	333.37	0.00	333.37	0.00		349.14

(See the reverse side for additional information)
IMPORTANT: RETAIN THIS STATEMENT FOR YOUR INVESTMENT AND TAX RECORDS

FORM P903 (10.93)

156

you see 25.7178. That's the number of shares Will had in the plan before the most recent dividend was reinvested.

This is the last of four statements Will received in 1993. On October 1 a total of $86.45 in dividends was used to purchase more stock; $81.37 was from the 412 shares outside the plan, $5.08 from the shares inside the plan. There was no service charge to buy the new shares, so 100 percent of the dividend went to work for Will. The price per share was 17.5038, and 4.9407 shares were acquired (4.6987 plus 0.2902). After the dividends were reinvested, Will owned 30.6567 shares within the DRP.

This company will automatically reinvest dividends each quarter, and there are no commissions or other charges. The company absorbs them for you. That's one great benefit of participating in DRPs. Many companies pick up the entire commission tab. Even if they don't, using a DRP is still a good deal because the commissions (and other charges) are far less than you'd pay a broker, especially on a small amount of money like $86 per quarter.

Most companies with DRPs also offer OCPs—optional cash payment plans. The company in this example does, too. About one-third down from the top of the form note the sentence "To make an optional cash payment, please detach and mail with your check." You tear off the top of the form and send it in with your money. OCPs have minimum and maximum amounts that can be contributed each quarter. The minimum is typically $25–$50 while the maximum can be $1,000, $2,000, and more.

Each quarter when this statement comes in, we have the option (but we don't have to exercise it) to mail as little as $25 or as much as $3,000 to the address shown and buy more shares of stock for Will. As with reinvested dividends, this company also pays the commission. If we send in $1,000 the entire $1,000 goes to work for my son, not a broker. If we buy more shares through the lowest-cost broker we can find, we're looking at $25 or more in unnecessary commissions.

Because of DRPs and OCPs, it's possible to begin a portfolio with as little as $500 and still invest in five different companies. The technique I'm discussing here is especially useful for a young person or anyone else who can only afford to start small. Let's assume twenty-year-old Mary saves $50 a month for ten months to accumulate $500. She picks five AFC companies with dividend reinvestment plans, each in a different industry. For simplicity, let's also assume each company sells for $50 per share and the commission to buy one share is also $50. Mary plunks down $500, $250 of which buys five shares of stock. The other $250, half her money, goes to the broker. This is not a good deal for Mary if she keeps investing $500 at a time because the broker will be taking half. But it is when she utilizes the OCPs.

Mary makes sure the one share of each of the five companies is registered in her name (not in "street" name, meaning it is held by the broker) and delivered to her. She then signs on for each company's dividend reinvestment plan. After the companies pay their next quarterly dividends, Mary will receive five statements that look similar to Will's statement. Almost without question, all her companies will have optional cash payment plans, and those will show on the fronts of the statements.

Before making her initial purchases, Mary should call each company (phone numbers are in the appendix) and ask for DRP and OCP information. She'll want to know about service fees and commissions, if any, and minimum-maximum limits for the OCPs. About 10 percent of the thousand companies offering DRPs charge a service fee. In most cases, they're capped at $3.00 and are little more than a nuisance. As the number of shares owned grows larger, the service fee shrinks as a percent of the dividends reinvested. Even so, if you're working with a small amount of money, the charges from some companies might make quarterly reinvestment a bad deal.

Mary will also want to inquire whether buying one share of stock is enough to open a company's DRP. If not, there are plenty of AFC companies that only require one share to begin. Those are the companies you should stick with.

For years, one of America's Finest Companies, Bristol-Myers Squibb, would allow investors to begin a DRP with just one share of stock. They could also buy additional shares with their cash dividends without paying a fee or brokerage commission. Stock purchases up to $3,000 per quarter were also free of fees or commissions. Then the company had a change of heart. It set a fifty-share minimum to participate in the DRP and also initiated a charge on shares purchased through the plan, and another charge when the shares are sold.

Mary continues to save $50 per month. After two months she has $100 to be mailed to the first of the five companies for investment. After two more months, she mails another $100 to the second, and so forth. At the end of twelve months, $600 is invested—$200 in the first company and $100 apiece in companies two through five.

The next $100 goes into the second company, and the cycle continues.

After two years, the portfolio will be out of balance because one or more of the stocks will have done better than the others. That's easy to correct. Mary adjusts her optional cash payments to buy a little more of the stocks that have gone up the least and a little less of the ones that have gone up the most. As she gradually increases her savings from $50 to $60 to $70 and more per month, she increases the size of the extra cash payments. All the while she's paying no commission dollars to a broker. Her companies are picking up all, or most, of the transactions costs. As Mary continues her dollar-cost averaging program through the years, she'll save hundreds, if not thousands, in commissions. All those saved dollars will be working for her.

When I started an investment program for Will in 1992, his mother and I invested roughly $5,000 in each of five different AFC companies. Total commissions were $621 through our full-service broker. As we invest an additional $5,000 per company, we'll save the entire $621 because Will's companies will absorb the costs. Since Will is only five, the $621 we don't spend—and which should compound at 13–15 percent annually—will grow to a minimum of $950,163 and a maximum of $2,722,463 by the time Will is 65. Staggering, isn't it?

There are drawbacks to dividend reinvestment plans whether they have the optional cash-payment feature or not. One is you can't instantly sell the shares held in the plan. You have to detach part of the quarterly DRP form and mail it back to the company or the financial institution administering the plan. With one of Will's companies, you'd have three options: (1) a stock certificate in your name for some of the shares in the plan (you name the amount); (2) a stock certificate in your name for all shares in the plan and your participation terminated; (3) your plan participation terminated by selling all and partial shares at the next available date, then the proceeds mailed to you. If the shares were in a brokerage account, you could sell them and get the money in a few days, sometimes the same day. With a DRP it will take weeks.

I own shares in a DRP that won't sell them for me. They'll mail me a certificate for all or some of the shares if I ask. Then I have to take the certificate to my broker to sell them. All that takes time and effort on my part.

When you want to buy shares of a company, you simply call your broker and buy them. In an OCP it can take weeks for the company to invest your money. Why? Because the company pools everyone's OCP contributions and buys only at certain times of the year. Your money and everyone else's sits idle in an omnibus account without earning interest until investment day arrives. That's bad. What's good is buying in "bulk" allows a company to keep commission expenses minimal.

Another drawback to a DRP is you need to save the final quarterly statement of each company each year for tax purposes. It will show all four quarterly transactions and the amount of dividends reinvested. Otherwise you won't know how much you paid for the shares. One trap a lot of investors fall into is they pay taxes twice on reinvested dividends. First, they pay taxes on dividends in the year they were reinvested. If they fail to add those reinvested dividends back to the cost of the original shares and "step up" their cost basis, they'll pay taxes on the dividends again when the shares are sold because the capital gain will be larger than it should be.

If you participate in a lot of DRPs, as some investors do, you'll never have an accurate picture of the value or balance of your portfolio unless you calculate it. And you won't be able to use DRPs for your retirement plan. That's because a financial institution has to domicile the account and hold all your securities in street name. When they're in street name, you can't participate in DRPs.

Fortunately, three brokerage firms have made investing in DRPs easier than ever. Charles Schwab, Smith Barney, and Merrill Lynch (others will eventually follow) are the ones I know that allow investors to participate in the dividend reinvestment plans of approximately four thousand companies, whether those companies have DRPs in place or not. A terrific benefit is that retirement plans are included. Schwab is the nation's largest discount broker, whereas Merrill Lynch is the largest full-service firm. Smith Barney is full-service as well.

Rather than go into detail about the dividend reinvestment services of these three excellent firms, I will point out one significant difference. Smith Barney charges modest commissions for quarterly dividend reinvestment. Schwab's program is free. Merrill Lynch charges nothing if you have their CMA (cash management account). I suggest you contact any one or all and tell them you want their information packets. Their phone numbers are given in Chapter 10.

There are many advantages to reinvesting dividends through a brokerage account rather than company by company. First, you can add the awesome power of dividend reinvestment for your retirement plan as well as for a taxable account. Second, you'll get one monthly statement (rather than quarterly statements from individual companies) showing the value of each stock and the amount of dividends reinvested. It's much easier to keep your portfolio balanced when all your holdings are together. It's easier at tax time, too, because all transactions are on one statement, not several.

Third, if you happen to lose one of your brokerage statements, it's easy to get a replacement by calling your account executive. I can get a copy from my broker by fax the same day I request it. If you lose a company's DRP statement, it's sometimes difficult to get another copy. More than one phone call or letter may be required.

Fourth, there are so many more companies from which to chose. I don't know the exact number of companies offering DRPs, but there are estimates ranging from nine hundred to eleven hundred. I usually say about a thousand. By going through a broker for dividend reinvestment, you can choose from close to four thousand companies.

Since I want you to invest only in America's Finest Companies, having four thousand choices compared with one thousand isn't the optimum benefit. The optimum is you can reinvest quarterly dividends in virtually all 417 of America's Finest Companies in either a taxable account, a nontaxable account, or even better, both. There's an easy way to find out which AFC companies qualify; just ask the broker before making your purchases. If an AFC company you like isn't in their group of four thousand or so, substitute another that is. Then tell the broker you think it should be.

The main disadvantage of a dividend reinvestment brokerage account is you can't participate in optional cash payment plans. You'll always have to pay a commission to add to your holdings. To me that isn't a great detriment, but it may be to you. Is the convenience and ease of record keeping worth more than the commission costs? Only you can decide.

One way to handle this dilemma is to make taxable investments through individual dividend reinvestment plans and use OCPs to save commissions. Make nontaxable investments through a broker offering dividend reinvestment for retirement plans. Even though you won't get the benefit of OCPs, you will be able to reinvest dividends and add compounding power to your portfolio.

Earlier in the chapter I mentioned that twenty-seven AFC companies allow you to reinvest dividends and make optional cash payments at discounts to market value ranging from 2.5 percent to 5 percent. The discounts are taxable as ordinary income. The twenty-seven are shown here alphabetically with their discounts.

American Heritage Life	5%
American Water Works	5
Ball Corporation.	5
BB&T Financial	5
CNB Bancshares	3
Colonial Gas	5
Connecticut Water Service	5
Empire District Electric	5
EnergyNorth	5
First Michigan Bank	5
First of America Bank	5
Fuller, H.B.	3
Great Western Financial	3
Green Mountain Power	5

Household International   2.5
Huntington Bancshares   5
Mercantile Bankshares   5
Middlesex Water   5
NationsBank   5
New Plan Realty Trust   5
NC Natural Gas   5
Piedmont Natural Gas   5
Public Service of NC   5
Telephone & Data Systems 5
United Cities Gas   5
UtiliCorp United   5
Valley Resources   5

Gradually, more and more companies are allowing you to make the initial share purchase through them rather than a broker. The seventeen AFC companies allowing direct purchases are:

American Recreation Centers
American Water Works
Atlantic Energy
Central & South West Corp-
    oration
Duke Power
Exxon Corporation
Florida Progress
Hawaiian Electric
Johnson Controls

Madison Gas & Electric
Minnesota Power & Light
National Fuel Gas
    Company
Regions Financial Corpo-
    ration
SCANA Corporation
Union Electric
WICOR
Wisconsin Energy

To learn the specifics of their programs, call the companies in which you're interested and ask how to make direct purchases of their stock.

CHAPTER NINE

How to Dodge Uncle Sam Outside Your Retirement Plan

You've got to hand it to the IRS. If you don't, they'll come get it.

—ANONYMOUS

Money inside a retirement plan receives preferential treatment because it grows without taxes until withdrawn. If you sell appreciated stock in your retirement plan, there will never be any capital-gains taxes to pay. Taxes are paid only when money is withdrawn, beginning as early as fifty-nine and a half and no later than seventy and a half.

Money outside a retirement plan is treated poorly by both Uncle Sam and all the states with income taxes. Taxes on dividends and capital gains must be paid in the years they're realized. Although losses can be used to offset gains, that's not much of a benefit, because taxes can knock an iceberg-size hole in your financial ship. Let me show you what I mean, using my eighty-two-year-old father, Harold, as the example.

My father was a banker all his working life. When he retired from Wachovia Corporation in 1972, his largest asset by far was (and still is) shares of Wachovia stock. Wachovia is one of the most profitable major banks in the country and also is one of America's Finest Companies. Excellent management is one of Wachovia's hallmarks. Current CEO L. M. Baker, Jr., is only the sixth since the company was founded in the 1800s. The stock has been a stellar performer since my father started buying it decades ago. From 1976 through the end of 1993, the compound annual return was a little more than 17 percent. As a result, he has substantial capital gains in a lot of his holdings. What would happen if he decided to sell one thousand shares?

The current price of Wachovia is 38, so he'd sell the thousand shares for $38,000, less commissions of about $400. Some of his stock has a cost basis of about $5 per share. If he sold this portion, the capital gain would be roughly $32,600. In a combined 35 percent tax bracket (28 percent federal and 7 percent state), Uncle Sam and North Carolina would take $11,410, leaving him with $26,190 of the original $38,000. Thirty-one percent of my father's principal would disappear.

If he reinvested the $26,190 in another stock, it would

have to rise 45 percent in price ($38,000 divided by $26,190) to get back to the initial $38,000, the amount the one thousand shares were worth before he took a profit. If Wachovia was in a retirement plan, my father could sell and pay no taxes, only the $400 in commissions. Unfortunately it's not. That's why he never sells. He doesn't want to pay taxes. I don't blame him, even though his portfolio is lopsided because there's so much Wachovia. Luckily for him it's been an abnormally good performer.

Capital-gains taxes can take a huge chunk out of profits in a taxable account. That's why it makes the most sense to lock away every investment dollar possible in a retirement plan. For one thing, the government makes it hard to get money out of a retirement plan without triggering a 10 percent penalty. If you're building a stock portfolio for something other than life after work, you'll probably do it in a taxable account. Then you can get your hands on your money penalty-free anytime you want to.

To minimize taxes, you have to build a portfolio of low- to no-yielding (2 percent down to 0 percent) stocks and sell rarely. Selling rarely (and therefore not paying capital-gains taxes) is what has allowed many self-made millionaires and billionaires, members of the Forbes 400, to establish such incredible fortunes—Warren Buffett of Berkshire-Hathway, Leon Levine of Family Dollar Stores, Leslie Wexner of The Limited, to name three. Fortunately, doing what they've done is an easy task with American's Finest Companies as your investment partner. There are 112 stocks, roughly one-fourth of the 417-stock universe, that yield no more than 2 percent. Forty-three yield 1 percent or less, and 13 yield nothing at all.

Last fall an attorney client, who's very well-to-do, flew

down from Baltimore for one of my personal-coaching sessions. He already had a substantial buildup in his retirement plan and was making the maximum annual contribution each year, but he still could put a lot of extra money into his taxable portfolio. The portfolio contained a lot of low-quality stocks sprinkled with America's Finest Companies like Merck. There were capital gains in some issues, losses in the others, and no particular rhyme or reason as to what would be purchased and sold. In addition, there were far too many stocks to keep up with. My recommendation was to sell most of the stocks, offset the gains with the losses, and assemble a portfolio of ten of America's Finest Companies, with 10 percent of the money in each. The client and I together chose the portfolio, and the end result was one we felt comfortable with.

Without revealing what he bought, I'll show you the thought process that went into picking the ten names. You may or may not be, but my client is in a high tax bracket. With state and federal taxes combined, dividend income is taxed at approximately 45 percent. Because the combined rate is so high, it will pay my client to focus on low- or no-yielding stocks and strive for capital gains rather than dividend income. If you want to invest in stocks for a combination of yields and capital gains (utilities, for example), those stocks should be in your retirement plan, where dividends won't be taxed. When you invest outside the retirement plan, the focus should be on capital application at the expense of yield.

A general rule of thumb is that companies whose stocks have low yields (McDonald's) or no yields (Toys "R" Us) grow faster than their counterparts with higher yields.

This is not inviolate when applied to individual companies, but for our purposes it's a good guideline when applied to companies on the whole. The reason it works is faster-growing companies figure they can earn more for shareowners by plowing earnings back into the businesses rather than paying it in dividends. Said another way, faster-growing companies earn higher returns on reinvested dollars than the typical company or investor. Slower-growing industries like banking and utilities provide above-average dividend yields because their growth prospects aren't nearly so bright as for a Wal-Mart or a Nucor.

The twenty-five top-performing stocks among AFCs over the past ten years (from capital appreciation) were, as a group, very low yielding stocks. Several, including Clayton Homes and Biomet, paid no dividends at all. The rest had minuscule dividend yields compared with the entire AFC universe. Since capital gains is what we're looking for in a taxable portfolio, below-average-yielding stocks must make up the portfolio.

It's easy to pick such a portfolio and takes no more than a couple of minutes. Turn to the alphabetical listing of companies in the appendix and start skimming the list. For this example I'm sticking with all companies yielding no more than 2.0 percent and want to end up with eight.

I see Automatic Data Processing, a computer software company, with a 1.1 percent yield. ADP is near the top of the AFC heap, with forty-four back-to-back years of higher earnings and twenty-seven of dividends, the fifth-best record of all companies. Even more amazing, the company has posted 131 straight quarters of double-digit earnings growth. Although I can't prove it, that has to be the best record in the world. I know it's the best in this country.

I don't want more than one company starting with an A (you can have more than one if you like) so I skip to the Bs and find Bandag (auto parts) is the first B company meeting the 2.0 percent yield criterion at 1.3 percent. Bandag has one of the strongest balance sheets in the AFC universe, with equity being more than 70 percent of total assets. Then I go to the Cs. There, Century Telephone yields 1.2 percent.

In the Ds I find R. R. Donnelley & Sons, a printing company, with a 1.9 percent yield. The first company in the Es, Eaton Vance (financial industry), has a 2.0 percent yield and thirteen years in a row of higher dividends per share. First Empire State, a bank, yields 1.3 percent. First Empire is in the financial industry, but Eaton Vance is a mutual-fund company. If they seem to be too close to being in the same industry, pass by First Empire State and move on to FlightSafety International, a commercial-services company serving the airline industry with a 1.1 percent yield.

Now I have six companies and need only two more to get to eight. GEICO, a multiline insurance company, is first in the Gs meeting my criterion and sports a 2.0 percent yield. To round out the list, I spot Hannaford Brothers, a food wholesaler with a terrific earnings and dividend record and a 1.6 percent yield. I have the eight companies I need and spent less than two minutes coming up with them.

Now I buy the portfolio and invest 12.5 percent of my money in each. One year from the purchase date, I add additional money to the portfolio and bring the bottom

COMPANY	INDUSTRY	YIELD
Automatic Data Processing	Computer software	1.1%
Bandag	Auto parts	1.3
Century Telephone	Communications	1.2
R. R. Donnelley & Sons	Printing	1.9
Eaton Vance	Financial	2.0
FlightSafety International	Commercial services	1.1
GEICO Corporation	Multiline insurance	2.0
Hannaford Brothers	Food wholesaling	1.6
	Average	1.4%

two or three laggard positions into line with the others. If one stock, let's say it's Bandag, runs way ahead of the rest of the pack and becomes dramatically overweighted, I don't sell part of it to bring it into line with the other seven because I don't want to pay capital-gains taxes. I let my profits ride. As long as I don't realize them, my money continues to grow tax-deferred with the exception of taxes I'll pay on annual dividends. That won't be a lot because the yield is a skimpy 1.4 percent.

If I want to pay no taxes, I need eight companies that don't pay dividends. They're just as easy to find as stocks with meager yields although there aren't nearly as many from which to choose. In this example I'll start with the As and skim the list alphabetically. The first no-dividend payer is Biomet in the medical products industry. Next is Buffets. They're followed by Citizens Utilities in the utility industry and Clayton Homes in manufactured housing.

Company number five is Crown Cork & Seal (containers). Number six is King World Productions in leisure; number seven, Microsoft Corporation, computer software; number eight, Nichols Research.

COMPANY	INDUSTRY
Biomet	Medical products
Buffets, Inc.	Restaurant
Citizens Utilities	Utility
Clayton Homes	Manufactured housing
Crown Cork & Seal	Containers
King World Productions	Leisure
Microsoft Corporation	Computer software
Nichols Research	Electronics

What could be easier? I quickly assembled a great portfolio of eight companies, each in a different industry, and they pay no dividends. This is a totally tax-deferred portfolio—just like a retirement plan—so long as I never sell and take a capital gain. One big advantage is I have instant access to my money in case I need it. There's no early-withdrawal penalty as there is with a retirement plan.

In a taxable account, there are only two good reasons ever to sell one of your stocks. The first is if the stock is deleted from a future edition of this book. In that case you sell the deleted stock and replace it with another America's Finest Company. The second reason to sell is that you need the money. Other than these, there isn't a good reason to sell unless one of your stocks has a loss, and you'd like to use the loss to offset other income. In a nontaxable account, the loss wouldn't be recognized.

It's important for you always to picture yourself as a buyer, not a seller, especially in a taxable account. Once your portfolio is set up, you want to keep buying more of what you've got and keep all stock positions in as near equal proportion as possible. Sell only when necessary. Otherwise Uncle Sam (and probably the state where you reside) will come calling to claim his "fair" share of *your* profits. Why pay taxes when you don't have to? Avoid them by letting your portfolio continue to appreciate over the next five, ten, fifteen, twenty years or more.

Multibillionaire Warren Buffett is a buyer of quality, and he rarely sells. Since he's worth more than $8 billion and is one of the world's wealthiest individuals, what he knows is worth knowing. Buffet says, "Buying only the best is something that . . . is very simple and very obvious." He also says his favorite holding period is "forever."

If you invest strictly in America's Finest Companies and continue to buy more of what you own and rarely sell, then you are modeling Buffett, the finest example of a successful long-term investor. Maybe you won't be worth $8 billion before you die (then again maybe you will), but you could easily become a millionaire, even a multimillionaire, if you have enough time and patience.

To start building a secure financial future with a portfolio of America's Finest Companies, to continue buying them, and to hold them for a long time is such a simple (I call it a no-brainer) strategy you have to wonder why everyone doesn't do it.

CHAPTER TEN

If You've Never Invested Before, It's Easy to Get Started

If you've invested before, you've already got a brokerage account and know how it works and the commissions and fees involved. But if you're just beginning, the prospect of opening an account can be intimidating, particularly if you've got only a few hundred or a few thousand dollars to invest. You may think you're such a small investor nobody will want to do business with you. It's true a lot of brokers aren't interested in accounts that "small" because they think they don't make enough commissions. What a shortsighted view! These brokers fail to realize that large accounts usually don't start large; they start small. If one broker doesn't seem interested, hang up and try another one. There are plenty who will gladly accept your business, and they're not hard to find.

You can normally open an account with any stockbroker by phone. In just a few minutes you give the broker enough background information (nothing confidential or revealing) to activate your account and then place your initial order to buy shares of America's Finest Companies. Opening a new account is that simple, and costs nothing but a few minutes' time.

Discount brokers generally offer lower commission rates than full-service brokers because they're seeking investors who want to save money and who, like you, make their own investment decisions. Charles Schwab (800-435-4000) is the largest, but there are others with a national presence, including Quick & Reilly (800-221-5220), Olde Discount (800-USA-OLDE), Pacific Brokerage (800-421-8395), Waterhouse (800-765-5185), and Jack White & Co. (800-233-3411).

The good news about discount brokers is that more and more are cropping up around the country. Your bank may have a discount brokerage operation, as do quite a few of the banks in my hometown. If it does, you can get more information at any of the bank's branches. Many discounters are local, have rock-bottom commission rates, and advertise little if at all. They usually don't find you. You have to find them. A good place to start is the yellow pages.

Full-service national firms are led by Merrill Lynch (800-MER-RILL) and Smith Barney Shearson (212-698-

6000), the two brokers with the largest sales forces. They're trailed by a number of smaller but high-quality regional firms scattered across the country in cities like San Francisco, Dallas, St. Petersburg, Minneapolis, Atlanta, Charlotte, and Richmond. What all these firms have in common is they usually have the highest commissions and fees, but they also offer services the discounters don't offer, like stock and bond research. They also sell an array of financial products, including life insurance and annuities.

Since you're now your own money manager and are comfortable with your own decisions about what and when to buy and sell, where you open a brokerage account isn't nearly as important as it would be if you had no idea what you were doing. You do know what you're doing. You're in control, not the broker. There's no need to worry about a salesman selling you something you don't want because you won't let him.

What is important is that the firm is reputable and has the services you need. Just as important is how much they charge. Most brokers have a fixed minimum commission in the $25 to $50 range regardless of the transaction size. The average is about $40. If you buy one share of each of five stocks, total commissions could be as low as $100, as high as $250, and on average around $200. One of my clients wanted to buy $200 of stock for each of her four grandchildren and have the shares registered in their names. After a lot of shopping, she found the lowest commission rate at the discount-brokerage arm of her bank.

The *Fortune 1994 Investor's Guide* surveyed a number of national, regional, and discount brokers and found commissions on fifty shares of a $20 stock varied from an average of $234 for twelve of the national/regional brokers to $96 for the four discounters cited. Super-discounter Pacific Brokerage was by far the lowest at $25. For one hundred shares of a $30 stock, the range for all the brokers from high to low was $91 to $40, except for Pacific Brokerage, which came in again at $25.

Transaction fees are tacked onto commissions, and most brokers have them. They're in the $2–$4 range. Schwab doesn't. Neither does Quick & Reilly. There are also annual fees (roughly $50) for inactive accounts that are charged by some firms, plus annual IRA fees (about $40), which most firms make you pay. Schwab has no inactive account fee and assesses only $22 for a small IRA. For one with at least $10,000, there's no charge and never will be. That's their guarantee.

Almost every firm has a central asset account or something akin to it. With a minimum balance (usually $10,000, sometimes $20,000) you get a credit card and check-writing privileges. All cash in the account earns daily interest in each firm's money-market fund. Full-service firms assess annual fees in the $60 to $100 area. Discounters Schwab, Fidelity, Olde Discount, and Quick & Reilly assess nothing. Quick & Reilly's minimum balance is just $500; for the other three it's $5,000.

Now that you have a good idea what brokers offer and how much it costs to do business with them, I want to hone in on the three firms—Merrill Lynch, Smith Barney Shearson, and Charles Schwab—that provide quarterly dividend reinvestment on approximately four thousand companies for both taxable and retirement accounts. Since I'm such a huge proponent of automatic dividend reinvestment and want you to be, too, these firms deserve special mention.

Schwab's brochure says, "You can reinvest the dividends on any U.S. stock." Every dividend-paying stock in America's Finest Companies qualifies for dividend reinvestment at Schwab.

At Smith Barney all cash dividends on stocks designated by you are credited to your account the date they're paid. The dividends are then automatically debited from your account, and more shares (plus fractions of shares) are purchased the next business day. Smith Barney offers free dividend reinvestment for individual retirement accounts, which makes their IRAs attractive. For other types of accounts, a "modest" (their words) fee is charged, based upon the size of the dividend. For those with Financial Management Accounts, there's a preferential fee rate.

Dividend reinvestment is free at Charles Schwab, and it can apply to any Schwab account, including IRAs, Keoghs, trusts, or custodials.

Dividend reinvestment is also free at Merrill Lynch. But there's one stipulation: you must open a cash management account (CMA) that requires a minimum $20,000 balance with a $100-per-year fee. That may or may not be a problem for you. The firm's service, Reinvestment Power, is available for securities on the New York and American stock exchanges and Nasdaq stocks.

Merrill Lynch has a unique program for smaller investors that's worth mentioning, and it encourages automatic quarterly dividend reinvestment. I happened to find out about it by accident a few years ago. It's called The

Blueprint Program (800-637-3766) and through it "you can invest in stocks, mutual funds, and precious metals by the dollar amount. That means you can acquire fractions of shares or ounces, not just whole units."

Call Merrill's toll-free number, and they'll send you a brochure and application. If you want to sign up, send back the application with a check representing your initial investment. Minimum to start is only $500. The annual administrative fee is $30. When the application and check are received, your money will be invested on the next business day. To make additional stock purchases, money for the transactions must already be in the account via check or money order. In a regular brokerage account, you buy the stock first and then pay for it within five business days.

The brochure says, "you receive as much as 60% off regular Merrill Lynch fees for stock transactions," and you have the option to dollar-cost average by taking advantage of the Systematic Investment Plan. There's a $50 monthly or $100 quarterly minimum, which is very reasonable, and the payments can be drafted from a checking or savings account.

For dividend reinvestment there's a 4 percent transaction fee up to $100. Between $100.01 and $500.00 it's the greater of 2 percent or $4.00. From $500.01 and up it's a flat 1.5 percent. Commissions range from as little as $10 for transactions up to $200 to 1.15 percent plus $39.50 if you're at the $5,000.01–$7,500 level. There's also a $3.85 handling fee for each Blueprint transaction.

A lot of people don't like to talk with a broker because they're afraid he'll try to sell them something they don't want. By using The Blueprint Program, you avoid the broker. Instead, you talk to a customer-service rep, who will be a different person each time you call to place an order or ask for account information. Participants receive quarterly statements showing all purchases, sales, dividends, and dividends reinvested as well as the amount of money added to or taken out of the account.

When you begin an investment program with as little as $500, commissions, transaction fees, and other charges can be a real burden because they can take a good chunk out of principal. But as you continue to add to your portfolio every six months to a year and your assets multiply, they become less and less of an albatross. Although it's important to reduce or eliminate every cost possible, it's of far greater importance to have your portfolio invested strictly in America's Finest Companies, keep the holdings properly weighted and buy more of what you already own every chance you get.

In my twenty-four years in the investment business, I've seen people fail to make a lot of money because they spent so much time shopping for the best broker, or trying to unearth the best brokerage firm, or attempting to cut commissions to the bone, or all three. They were putting the cart before the horse, and that's not a profitable strategy. Investing for maximum profits requires patience, a simple strategy like the one unfurled in these pages, and at least a ten-year horizon to give the strategy ample time to work. Keeping costs minimal improves your overall return, there's no doubt about that, but it won't improve your return nearly so much as planning to beat Wall Street with America's Finest Companies, implementing your plan, and sticking to your plan.

CHAPTER ELEVEN

How to Turn Your Children or Grandchildren into Savvy Investors and Make Them Millionaires in the Process

The day after my daughter was born in 1978, I opened a custodial account for her at the brokerage firm where I was director of equity research. A custodial account is as simple to open as a regular brokerage account. An adult signs on as "custodian" until the child is eighteen, at which time the account is under the complete control of the child, who, of course, by then is a young adult. Anyone can contribute up to $10,000 of cash, securities, or a combination of the two to a custodial account every year with no gift-tax consequences.

Once the account was set up, my wife and I contributed a few thousand dollars, and then I made three very important phone calls, to my father, my mother, and my aunt, who's like a second mother. Since this was their first grandchild by me, I told them I was certain they'd each want to help secure Gracie's financial future with gifts of cash or stock. Naturally they couldn't say no. It wasn't long before those gifts came in the mail, and I was able to add several thousand dollars of stock to Gracie's account. Before she was even six months old, she had a five-digit sum in her brokerage account, which I invested in a portfolio of growth stocks. There was no America's Finest Companies back then, but I could still pick stocks to beat the market. I knew Gracie was off on a sound financial footing.

Since then my father and aunt have made some additional gifts of stock, but the account is worth what it is today (about $200,000) primarily because her portfolio has performed so well. I don't know how much money has been withdrawn to pay for private-school education, but she started in kindergarten and is now a junior. Average tuition taken out per year must have been at least $7,000, so you see the portfolio has been a real winner.

When my son, Will, was born in 1989, I immediately opened a custodial account for him as I did for his sister. Although he didn't get off to a five-digit start as she had done, he's still in excellent financial shape for a five-year-old. He attends a wonderful Montessori school, and his account is paying all tuition and miscellaneous expenses.

Once Gracie and Will are eighteen, the money in their accounts is theirs to do with as they please. That's the law as long as they're legally competent, and I have no reason to think they won't be. I hope they'll let me help them manage their money until they get through college, but they don't have to. Even though these accounts are for their education, they don't have to spend the assets for that purpose. They can dispose of them any way they wish once they're of age.

I want both my children to have secure financial futures. There should be more than enough money left over in their accounts after four years of college (perhaps graduate school, too) to be able to achieve that goal. Gracie will graduate from college in the spring of 2000. (I went on record in my newsletter in fall 1990 saying the Dow will be at 10000 by then. Let's hope I'm right.)

Assuming college expenses at a liberal $20,000 per year and 13 percent growth (before taxes) in the portfolio, she ought to have about $250,000 to work with when she graduates. If that money grows at a modest 9 percent a year after taxes and she doesn't tap into it, it will be worth close to $2.8 million when she's 50 and well over $6.5 million when she's 60. At 10 percent after tax, which is certainly achievable, the numbers will be $3.6 million at age 50 and nearly $9.5 million by age 60.

Although she could do it now as a minor with me as custodian, I'll encourage Gracie to open an IRA when she's 18 and put every dime she earns into it (up to $2,000 annually) while she's in college. When I was in school, I was fortunate to have my father pay all tuition and other expenses. The $3,000 or so I earned working for the student newspaper was mine to save or spend. Had I known anything about investing, I probably would have set at least part of it aside. Instead I spent it. That's okay. I had a lot of fun. If Gracie earns $100 per month nine months per year during her four years in college, and she invests it in an IRA compounding at 13 percent annually, that little $3,600 investment will swell to nearly $500,000 by the time she's 60. Even better, if she contributes the maximum $2,000 annually from age 22 through age 60, her IRA will multiply to $2.3 million.

An IRA is a powerful wealthbuilder for anyone, especially a child. The younger the child the more valuable the IRA is. Suppose five-year-old Will begins to do odd jobs like mowing lawns (as I did) when he's 10 and mows five each week during the summer (again as I did). I made $7 a week back in the 1950s. Will can probably make at least ten times that. Let's say he rakes in $75 weekly for ten weeks each summer, starting at age 10 and ending when he turns 16. At 16 he'll drive a car and be much "too old" to mow lawns. For each of the six years he works, Will will put the entire $750 into his IRA, which will earn 13 percent annually through age 65. That's only $4,500, but it will surge to $2.8 million over 49 years. Will will become a millionaire from mowing lawns for just six years. Since this money will be in an IRA, the principal will grow without being taxed until Will begins to withdraw it.

I assume Will will be like a lot of young people and want to spend most of his income. Or worse, he'll be like I was. I spent everything I earned and then asked (begged?) my parents and grandparents for more. The words *saving* and *investing* meant nothing to me. I want them to mean something for my children.

To offset Will's urge to spend what he earns while in high school, I'll offer to match it. It will be either a dollar-for-dollar match or a two-for-one match, probably the latter. Under a two-for-one match, for every dollar Will invests in his IRA I'll give him a dollar to spend as he wishes. I'll also invest a dollar in his custodial account. While he's putting $4,500 from mowing lawns into his IRA, I'll be pumping $4,500 into his custodial account. Using a conservative aftertax return of 9 percent, the $4,500 from me will be worth $306,981 when he is 65. But if I invest all the money in non-dividend-paying stocks and sell rarely and the money grows at 13 percent like the IRA, it will grow to about $1.8 million. With my small gifts and Will's small contributions to his IRA, he'll amass close to $4.6 million by age 65.

If I were to sit in a room with parents and grandparents and we discussed whether they should provide for their children's financial security, assuming they are able to, there'd probably be a heated argument within a few minutes. Some would say providing financial security works to a child's detriment because the child doesn't learn how to fend for himself in the real world. I recently met a father, Eddie, who feels exactly like that. He grew up poor and worked hard all his life to make ends meet. His house is paid for, he still manages to set aside a little extra money each month, and he and his wife like to junket to Las Vegas and Atlantic City regularly to enjoy, in his words, "the good life." When I asked Eddie about his children, he said he planned to leave nothing to them. It was up to them to "work hard and provide for themselves" just as he's done. That's one view.

Another is that parents and grandparents should offer some financial aid but should not try, even if they can afford it, to provide everything monetary a child needs. And still a third view is my view. I want to make my children as financially comfortable as I can before they enter the workplace, which I assume both will do eventually. Why? Because I'd like both of them to have the opportunity to enjoy the kinds of careers they can sink their teeth into and not have to worry about whether the job pays enough. I want Will to become a high school history teacher if that's what he really wants, even though teachers, in my opinion, are grossly underpaid for what they render to society. If Gracie wants to be an artist, I don't want her to "starve" while she pursues her dream.

Using my children as examples, I'm demonstrating the relative ease with which all children can build small fortunes, even large ones. They can do so without your help if they have the knowledge within these pages, but it will be considerably easier with your assistance. A custodial account at a brokerage is a great starting place. If you're worried that your children or grandchildren will be foolish with their money after they reach 18, you can, for modest fees, establish trust accounts that are very flexible yet have restrictions preventing the assets from being abused. You can be the trustee and invest the money however you like. In either a custodial or a trust account, you'll want to invest strictly in America's Finest Companies. If your child or grandchild is eight or older, he or she will most likely want to participate in assembling the portfolio. Sometimes children even younger than that willingly cooperate. All you need do is ask them.

Remember the example of my daughter, who invested in eight companies she chose herself in 1988. Through September 30, 1994, they've beat the S & P 500 by 75 percent. Gracie was excited about having the chance to pick companies. She wasn't interested in why she was doing it. She just knew it was fun. Money is fun to most children and young people (as it should be with us adults), so why not take advantage of that?

As I said in a previous chapter, I teach applied economics to juniors and seniors at my daughter's school. By the time she takes this excellent course as a senior, I will have taught it seven times. I hope she'll enjoy it and not be embarrassed around her dad. I'm the real-life "consultant" who takes practical experiences and knowledge into the classroom to bring economics to life for these bright young adults. Junior Achievement writes its own economics text, which is revised and updated every three years. If you've ever hankered to learn more about the "dismal science" but couldn't find an interesting, readable text, JA's is it. It's the most useful economics text I've ever studied.

With every group of students, I spend two to three sessions on investing, using the principles outlined here. One exercise I emphasize is having them pick five companies they'd like to invest in. There are only three rules. One, the companies must be high quality. Two, they must have dividend reinvestment plans. The students don't know whether the companies have DRPs or not, so they keep picking until they come up with five that do. Three, they have to hold these companies for twenty years. They cannot sell (unless there's a buyout and they're forced to) during the period, but they can buy more of the stocks whenever they get additional money.

Each of the five classes I've worked with to date has picked a good portfolio. Not surprisingly, at least to me, they always choose five companies in different industries. I don't tell them to. They do it as if by instinct. Most of the companies over the past five years have been among

America's Finest Companies, even though the students haven't known which are in the universe and which aren't.

McDonald's, PepsiCo or Coca-Cola, Kmart or Wal-Mart, and Merck or Bristol-Myers Squibb have been popular choices. My latest class started with ten companies initially and then narrowed the list to five. Half the ten were AFC companies. Any of your children or grandchildren could come up with a similar list of ten to twelve names. My bet is there will be at least five or six AFC companies, maybe more. All you need to do is eliminate the ones that aren't in AFC and let the child buy five of the ones that are, as long as they're in different industries. If there aren't enough, keep working until you have five spread among five industries, each with a dividend reinvestment plan. It won't take long.

A five-stock portfolio is easily put together at very little cost. Let's say the child wants to buy McDonald's, Coca-Cola, Colgate-Palmolive, Quaker Oats, and William Wrigley Jr. All have DRPs and you need buy only one share of each to begin participating. One broker you can call to execute your orders is Dean Witter. The firm has a flat 10 percent commission rate on small transactions. If you buy one share of each of these five, you'll spend about $250, less total commissions around $25, based on prices at this date. Get the shares registered in the child's name, with you or another adult as custodian, and have them delivered to your home. Each company will mail a simple form so you can check the block required to participate in the company's divided reinvestment plan. Additional share purchases can be made through the companies' optional investment plans (OCPs), which generally carry no com-mission, or a small one at worst.

To make the investing process even more fun for the child, you should know that a number of companies offer freebies to shareholders. Several years ago I bought one share of Quaker Oats and had the lone share delivered to me. Each quarter I receive a $0.53 dividend check and four coupons for Quaker products worth $2.00. That's $8.00 in coupons per year. After three years of owning one share, I had gotten my money back in coupons alone.

Coupons might not be too exciting to a child, but how about a box of chewing gum? Every December, Wrigley sends all shareholders a box of twenty five-stick packs of gum hand-picked by Mr. Wrigley himself. Hershey Foods has a toll-free number shareowners can use to order gifts for friends and relatives. Anheuser-Busch has a Theme Parks Club for shareholders allowing 10–15 percent dis-counts at the country's facilities scattered across the coun-try. To be eligible for these perks, the shares must be registered in the name of the shareholder and cannot be held by a broker.

If your child or grandchild loves to bowl, consider American Recreation Centers. An investor has to own a lot of shares—five hundred—but that amount entitles the owner (who automatically becomes a Distinguished Share-holder Club member) to five free games of bowling per day at any of the firm's alleys. The company owns Right Start children's catalog, and club members get 20 percent off all merchandise.

Colgate-Palmolive's new shareowners get a packet of discount coupons, which may or may not be fun for a child to receive. This will depend on the age of the child and what the coupons are for, but I guarantee the parent or grandparent will find them useful. Ditto for H. J. Heinz. CSX owns the world-famous Greenbrier resort. Shareholders can stay there at discounted rates. Minnesota Mining & Manufacturing sends its new shareholders a variety of Post-It notes, tape, and other accessories, while Kimberly-Clark provides the chance to buy a bag of its products at well off the regular retail price.

I'd never suggest buying one of these companies just for its perks, but the perks do make ownership more fun, especially for children. Children have to have fun while they're learning to invest. Otherwise they won't be interested. And come to think of it, having fun while you invest isn't a bad idea for adults either. Beating Wall Street with America's Finest Companies is the most fun way I know.

CHAPTER TWELVE

How to Use America's Finest Companies Statistics for Maximum Profits

This book shows you a simple, time-proven way to make your money grow at an above-average rate with practically no risk. By investing solely in America's Finest Companies, you can safely double your money every five to six years and beat 75 percent of all investment professionals 100 percent of the time.

As I pointed out in Chapter 1, a diversified portfolio of America's Finest Companies should give you a 13–15 percent compound annual return compared to 12 percent, the market's rate for the past fifty years. That 1–3 percent advantage over a long period of time is worth hundreds of thousands of extra dollars.

If you invest $50 per month at 12 percent for your child at birth and continue through age 18, his money will grow to $38,272 as the 19th birthday approaches. With no additional contributions from you or the child, that $38,272 will be worth $1,438,328 when he or she is 50; $4,467,228 at age 60; and $13,874,532 by age 70. These are staggering numbers, aren't they? You're probably asking yourself, "But isn't $13,874,532 at age 70 more than enough for anyone?" My answer is "It would sure be more than enough for me, by many millions."

My mission is to try to have you earn as much money as you can on your investments, as safely as you can, and in as little time as you can. I'd rather see you earn 13 percent per year than 12 percent. Fourteen percent would be even better and 15 percent even better than that. I believe 13–15 percent is reasonable. Beyond that, we go into the never-never land of returns that may never materialize, but are frequently promoted by others in the financial arena.

Why not earn as much money as possible? The more you earn, the more you'll have to spend on things you need, things you want, and for helping others, too. I'm not unreasonable or impractical. I know most of us don't save and invest every extra dollar and never spend it. We save and invest, or at least try to, in a manner that lets us spend part of our principal each year while leaving the balance to grow for the future.

Let's go back to the previous example, in which no money is withdrawn until at least age 50, and develop another example that mimics real life. In this instance, the young person is worth $38,272 when he's 18 and needs some money from his account for college, $8,000 per year for four years. The parents make up the difference. After taking out $8,000 for first-year expenses, $30,272 is left to grow at 12 percent, the market's historic return, until the next year, when another $8,000 is withdrawn, and so forth until the four years are complete. At graduation, the young adult is now 22 and his stockpile has shrunk to $17,399. This amount builds at 12 percent compounded annually. If nothing else is taken out, it will be worth $415,555 when he's 50; $1,290,651 when he's 60; and $4,008,569 when he's 70. But in reality, more will probably be extracted at some point. Maybe it's when he reaches 45 and buys the house of his dreams.

From age 22 to age 45, $17,399 at 12 percent will increase to $235,797. With $150,000 used to purchase the dream home (there'd be a mortgage for the balance), there's $85,797 to grow at a 12 percent annual rate. Five years later at age 50, it has grown to $151,204; to $469,616 at 60; and $1,458,554 at age 70. As a practical matter, money will likely be taken out at various other points from ages 45 to 70, so the end amount may or may not be close to $1,458,554.

If I repeat this illustration, using 13 percent and 15 percent returns, at the end of four years of college the remainder amounts are $18,559 and $20,999, respectively, compared with $17,399. At age 45, after $150,000 is used for the home, $158,574 and $372,696 are left over compared with $85,797. You can see what a huge difference these higher rates are making, even using 13 percent, a figure that's only one percent above the market's 12 percent.

In Chapter 8, I said I invested roughly $5,000 (plus commissions) per stock in five different stocks on February 7, 1992, for my son, Will, who was then nearly three. All dividends have been reinvested since inception. To date, Will's portfolio has knocked down a better return than the market, using, naturally, America's Finest Companies. What I'm saying works in theory and, most important, in practice, too. I successfully invest for myself and my children and outpace the market virtually every year, using America's Finest Companies. You can do it, too.

Someone once said, "The easiest way to end up with a small fortune is to start with a large one." I've proved the opposite to be true. You can end up with a large fortune by beginning with as little as $50 each month and earning the market's rate of return. By outstripping the market, the fortune will be even larger.

Of course these "case-study returns" assume no taxes, but that's not uncommon. Taxes are excluded whenever returns are discussed, whether they be for the market, a mutual fund, or a portfolio manager. We all know taxes are impossible to avoid. They can be heavily reduced but never completely eliminated.

They also assume the investment program begins at birth. That's fine if you've got a baby or grandbaby, but it won't do you any personal good because you're almost certainly years, if not decades, behind. It's still not too late even if you're 50 and have done little or nothing for your future. Will an extra 1 to 3 percent per year really make a difference to your financial security? You bet!

To illustrate, you're already covered by a retirement plan at work but have extra money and decide to invest $2,000 each year in your IRA. If you equal the market and earn 12 percent annually, you'll have $39,309 after 10 years; $83,506 after 15; and $161,397 after 20. If you earn 13 percent, the numbers will be $41,628 in 10 years; $91,343 in 15; and $182,940 in 20. Using a 15 percent return, you'll have $46,699 at the end of 10 years; $109,435 in 15; and $235,620 at the end of 20 years.

Over a twenty-year period, the difference between a 12 percent and a 15 percent return is $74,223, 46 percent more. I'd say that's sizable, wouldn't you? The difference is even more dramatic if you have a SEP or Keogh and can kick in a lot more than $2,000 per year. What if the amount is $10,000 annually instead of $2,000 and you begin at age 50? At 12 percent per year, you'll build an $806,987 nest egg. At 13 percent, the nest egg will be $914,699. At 15 percent, it will be $1,178,101—$371,114 more than if you earned 12 percent.

Any way I've measured it, America's Finest Companies have substantially outperformed the market over the past ten years, which means they've whomped most of the pros, too, since the market indexes beat at least three-quarters of them year in and year out. It's easy to see why. Each of the 417 companies that qualify for listing has increased dividends and/or earnings for at least ten straight years. Three hundred ninety-four have done it with dividends alone; 95 have done it with earnings; and a select 73 have done it in both categories.

It's easy to explain how America's Finest Companies are above-average performers. They're growing, and the value of their businesses is on a consistent uptrend. As the values of the businesses rise, the stock prices rise also. They have to. Here's why.

Look at this staircase. It begins on the left of the page and rises one step at a time until it gets to the right side,

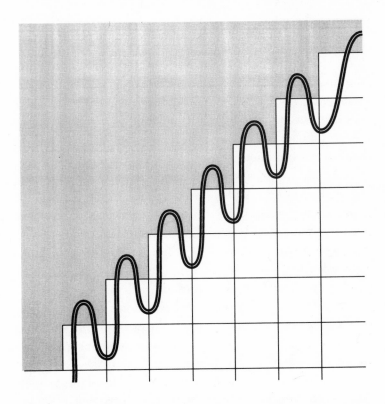

all the while getting taller and taller. This staircase could represent any of America's Finest Companies. Every step represents another increase in the value of the AFC company's business.

Now look at the curve. This represents an AFC stock price over the years. It goes up and down in value (randomly) in the short run, but the path is always in only one direction—upward. Sometimes the stock price is above what the company is really worth. At other times it's valued about correctly. And at still other times it's undervalued.

If you're dollar-cost averaging, as I strongly urge—purchasing the stock of an AFC company over five, ten, fifteen years, and more—you'll buy at different points along the stair steps. Maybe sometimes you'll pay too much. When you do, you'll buy fewer shares per dollar invested because the price is high. Often you'll buy shares on the cheap and for the same dollars invested will be able to load up. Given enough time, dollar-cost averaging will automatically produce superior results in contrast to a buy-and-hold strategy, as demonstrated in Chapter 7.

There are many ways to use the data here so that you end up with a well-balanced portfolio to meet your needs. You'll be a winner regardless of how you select your portfolio. Selecting can be as simple and easy as throwing darts. You could make copies of each of the statistical pages and post them on a wall you don't mind having a few holes in (in case you miss a throw or two). Next toss some darts, however many you require, one dart per company. Then buy the companies the darts strike.

One excellent portfolio you can buy outright or pick from is the ten Dow stocks (there are thirty that make up the venerable Dow Jones industrial average) that made the AFC cutoff. These are some of the oldest, strongest, most respected names in American industry. They've been around a long time, and you can rest assured they'll be around a lot longer. All have roots stretching back decades before the Great Depression, with the exception of McDonald's, the rookie of the group.

This is not only a well-diversified group of companies, it's a high-caliber group as well. Six of the ten are ranked A+ (highest) by Standard & Poor's, which establishes its rankings in a computerized system based on earnings and

COMPANY	YEARS OF HIGHER EARNINGS	YEARS OF HIGHER DIVIDENDS	S & P RANKING	DIVDS. PAID SINCE
Coca-Cola	19	31	A+	1893
DuPont	0	11	B+	1904
Exxon	1	11	B+	1882
General Electric	18	18	A+	1899
McDonald's	28	18	A+	1976
Merck and Company	0	18	A+	1935
Minnesota Mining & Manufacturing	2	35	A+	1916
J. P. Morgan	4	17	B+	1892
Philip Morris	0	28	A+	1928
Procter & Gamble	0	40	A–	1891

dividend records over the past decade. Stability is a key variable. One is A− (above average) and another three are rated B+ (average). I would never argue with Standard & Poor's, but I think they're too pessimistic on Exxon and J. P. Morgan.

From the end of 1983 through December 31, 1993, $1,000 spread equally among the ten stocks grew to $6,533 compared to $4,020 earned from an investment in Standard & Poor's 500 composite index. Money compounded at 20.6 percent in these AFC companies versus 15.0 percent for the market. That's the 3 percent difference I've been talking about. Actually, in this case it's 5.6 percent. Even if you'd owned the five worst performers (I bet you couldn't have done that if your life and all your money had depended on it), your return would have still beat the averages. You couldn't have picked the five top ones either short of a miracle, but if you had been fortunate enough to do that, your $1,000 would have multiplied to $8,367, 23.7 percent compounded annually.

It's easy to get together a portfolio using any one, or an assortment of, variables. If you want stocks that yield at least 4 percent, you have 122 from which to choose. Do you like stocks selling for $25 or less? There are 148. Or maybe you'd feel better owning only the companies ranked A+ by Standard & Poor's. You can choose them from the list in the appendix. Other selection criteria are industry, the price/earnings ratio, and the number of consecutive years of higher earnings and dividends.

You might like to make up your own combination of several variables, i.e., stocks priced between $20 and $40 per share, with P/E ratios no greater than 20, yields of

(1) COMPANY/STOCK SYMBOL	(2) INDUSTRY	(3) PRICE	(4) PRICE/ EARNINGS RATIO	(5) YIELD (%)	(6) DIVD. REINVEST. PLAN
Abbott Laboratories/ABT	Health Care	26	16.5	2.6	X

(7) CONSECUTIVE ANNUAL EARNINGS INCREASES	(8) CONSECUTI'E ANNUAL DIVIDEND INCREASES	(9) S & P RANKING	(10) ADDRESS/PHONE NUMBER
21	20	A+	One Abbott Park Rd., Abbott Park, IL 60064 312-937-6100

at least 3 percent, and at least fifteen years of higher dividends. It's up to you. The important thing to keep in mind is that however you build your portfolio, you're building it with the *crème de la crème* of corporations, the elite, America's Finest.

Now I'll tell you how to get more out of the data in the appendix. All the companies are listed alphabetically along with their stock symbols (column 1). An (A) follows a company's symbol if it trades, like Bowl America, Inc., on the American Stock Exchange.

After the stock symbol is the industry category in column 2. Regardless of the size of your stock portfolio—five, eight, ten, twelve, or more companies—each should be in a different industry. If you want to pick an eight-stock portfolio, there's no faster way than turning to any page of the company listings in the appendix and going down it company by company until you have the right number in diverse industries.

You could begin with Rochester Telephone (telephone). Rockwell International (aerospace) is right beneath it, followed immediately by Rohm & Haas Company (building materials). Skip RPM because it's also in building materials and go on to Rubbermaid (housewares), SAFECO (property insurance), Safety-Kleen (commercial services), and St. Joseph Light & Power (electric utility).

You'll also have to skip San Diego Gas & Electric because it, too, is a utility. Below that is Sara Lee Corporation (foods). With Sara Lee, you have eight companies in varied industries, and you only had to go through ten to find them. What could be easier? I realize all begin with either R or S, but if that doesn't bother you it doesn't bother me either. If all your companies have the same first letter in their names, it isn't a violation of any of my investing rules.

Column 3 shows the price of the stock when this book went to press. Column 4 gives the P/E ratio, which is the stock price divided by the latest twelve month's earnings. It's well documented that over longer periods of time a portfolio of stocks (culled from a large-enough group) with below-average price/earnings ratios consistently beats that group. For example, the eight lowest P/Es in the Dow Jones average regularly beat the Dow average of thirty stocks over one-, five-, and ten-year periods.

The first evidence I saw that this is true was in a paper written by Benjamin Graham, my financial hero. He cited research by the old brokerage firm of Drexel & Company in Philadelphia. Their 1965 study concluded that in twenty-two of the twenty-eight years since 1936 the ten lowest-P/E Dow stocks outdistanced the Dow.

In August 1991, I published the first annual directory of *America's Finest Companies*. Of the twenty-five lowest P/Es in that directory, twenty-four rose and only one fell in price over the next twelve months. The one stock that dropped plunged from 26 to 10. The remaining twenty-four advanced an average 36.7 percent (excluding dividends), compared with only 9.1 percent for the Dow Jones industrial average. They clobbered the Dow by a four-to-one margin. If you'd been lucky enough to own the top ten, you would have racked up an astonishing 57.8 percent from price appreciation.

The twenty-five lowest P/Es in the second annual edition were priced August 24, 1992. During the next twelve months, that group gained 30.7 percent versus 11.9 percent for the market, nearly a three-to-one margin of superiority. There were only two losers, and the five biggest movers rose a whopping 72.7 percent. The twenty-five lowest P/Es are listed below. They may not still be the lowest twenty-five by the time you read this.

Company	P/E
Bankers Trust NY Corp.	5.7
Sallie Mae	7.1
J. P. Morgan & Co.	7.5
National Security Group	7.7
Legg Mason Inc.	7.9
Washington Federal S&L	8.1
American National Insurance	8.3
Mercury General Corp.	8.3
Providian Corp.	8.4
Old Republic Intl.	8.4
USLIFE Corp.	8.4
Lincoln National Corp.	8.7
First of America Bank Corp.	8.7
Nichols Research Corp.	8.8
SAFECO Corp.	8.9
Republic New York Corp.	9.0
KeyCorp	9.0
Corestates Financial	9.2
Rochester Telephone Co.	9.2
Computer Data Systems	9.3
SCEcorp	9.4
Home Beneficial Corp.	9.4
Comerica Inc.	9.4
Eaton Vance Corp.	9.4
Dibrell Brothers Inc.	<u>9.5</u>
Average P/E	8.5

If you'd like to track America's Finest Companies yearly, including the lowest-P/E stocks, I invite you to become a charter member of America's Finest Investors and receive my monthly newsletter, plus a host of other benefits. There's a charter-membership application on page 257.

Column 5 shows the dividend yield for each stock if the company pays a dividend. Investing in stocks with above-average dividend yields is a conservative—but sound—way to make your money grow while simultaneously reducing downside risk and volatility. When you invest in the highest-quality companies like those shown in the back of the book and reinvest all your dividends, your returns will usually be equal to, or better than, the Dow Jones and S & P 500 indexes.

The twenty-five highest-yielding stocks on August 24, 1992, all yielded at least 6.1 percent, with the average coming in at 6.7 percent, more than twice the yield of the Dow or S & P 500 at the time. Although the two indexes went up more in value, the total return for the high-yielders was more than a percentage point better during the next year. Twenty-four out of twenty-five raised their dividends. Nevada Power did not and was cut from the AFC universe.

Column 6 shows whether a company has a dividend reinvestment plan. If the company reinvests dividends and optional cash payments at a discount to market price, the discount is shown in parentheses beside the X.

Columns 7 and 8 show the number of years of back-to-back earnings and dividend increases. Seventy-three companies, ranging from Abbott Laboratories and Albertson's to Wilmington Trust Corporation and William Wrigley Jr., have compiled double-digit increases in both categories. I haven't found any correlation between the length of a company's string of earnings and/or dividends and its stock price performance, but some people are more comfortable investing in companies with the longer records, like American Home Products, H&R Block, Emerson Electric, Johnson & Johnson, RPM, Rubbermaid, and Tootsie Roll Industries.

Column 9 provides the S & P rankings. The strongest companies are ranked B+ and higher although Standard & Poor's has no ranking for 16. More than half the 417 companies are in the B+ category or one above it. Eighty-two are classified A+, 99 as A, 106 as A−, and 93 as B+.

To contact a company for more information or to inquire about its DRP, use the address and phone number in column 10. If a toll-free number is available, it's included.

CHAPTER THIRTEEN

Chance Favors Only the Mind That Is Prepared

When my daughter was five, as my son is now, her favorite book was *The Value of Believing in Yourself: The Story of Louis Pasteur* by Spencer Johnson, M.D. (Few people know Johnson coauthored *The One-Minute Manager*.) It's one of my favorite books, too. I know his story almost by heart, having read it aloud several dozen times.

Pasteur (1822–95), as you may recall from your history courses, was a chemist and bacteriologist whose scientific exploits were widely ignored, since he was not a medical doctor. Pasteur had the firm conviction that diseases were caused by invisible enemies called germs or bacteria. Even though many of the finest minds in the world had no faith in his work, Pasteur believed in himself. He uncovered a cure for silkworm disease and later for anthrax and rabies. He also invented pasteurization, the process of heating milk to 140 degrees Fahrenheit for thirty minutes, then quickly cooling it.

Throughout the book, Louis Pasteur repeats to himself, "I believe I can. I believe I can" as he vigorously hunts for the rabies cure. He had to believe in himself because few others besides his wife, Marie, did. But Pasteur knew exactly what he was doing. Some of his critics refused to acknowledge his great works because they thought Louis Pasteur was just lucky. Pasteur knew luck had nothing to do with his outstanding accomplishments and said, "Chance favors only the mind that is prepared."

The average man or woman on the street thinks investing in stocks is nothing but a game of chance. The luckiest ones make money. The rest lose it. They don't realize that investing in stocks is the fastest way to accumulate wealth and that it can be done with virtually zero risk, as I've demonstrated. If you'll use the simple, rational method I've outlined, you'll have phenomenal success with your money regardless of the amount you begin with. In a sense, you'll be like Louis Pasteur because you'll ignore the advice commonly given by most financial experts, who want you to believe you need them to be successful. There aren't many of us who know you can do it yourself, have a lot of fun, and make a lot of money, too. Believe in yourself. You can do it!

In building a diversified portfolio of America's Finest Companies, you're doing far more than buying pieces of paper that change in price many times each day. You are actually buying pieces of American enterprises, the best this country has to offer. As these companies grow and thrive in the future, so will you by virtue of your ownership.

Does it really matter if the value of your shares goes down today and then bobs up tomorrow? Of course not. Value is not created in a day. Value takes years to build. Daily fluctuations in stock prices are meaningless. They do not affect the long-term value of the Finest Companies.

What does affect the value is growth in revenues, earnings, dividends, and the asset values of the businesses. If you continually add to your portfolio of first-rate companies, you can be certain that over the years the value will increase faster than from other investments—and keep you well ahead of inflation and the tax man, too.

There's nothing to wait for. You now have the knowledge you need for investing and stock-market success. Epicurus warned, "Life is wasted in procrastination." Procrastinate no longer. Start the steps to financial security today.

Happy investing!

Appendix:
List of
417 AFC
Companies

Company Name/Stock Symbol	Industry	Price	P/E	YIELD	Dividend Reinvestment Plan	Consecutive EPS Increases	Consecutive Dividend Increases	S&P Rank	Address/Phone Number
Abbott Laboratories/ABT	Health Care	28	15.8	2.7%	X	22	21	A+	One Abbott Park Rd., Abbott Park IL 60064 708/937-6100
ABM Industries/ABM	Comm. Services	19	12.8	2.7%	X	6	29	A-	50 Fremont St. #2600, San Francisco CA 94105 415/597-4500
AFLAC Inc./AFL	Insurance	34	13.7	1.4%	X	4	11	A	1932 Wynnton Rd., Columbus GA 31999 800/235-2667
Air Products & Chemicals Inc./APD	Chemicals	43	34.1	2.1%	X	0	11	A-	7201 Hamilton Blvd., Allentown PA 18195 215/481-4911
Albertson's Inc./ABS	Grocery	27	19.4	1.6%	X	24	22	A+	PO Box 20, Boise ID 83726 208/385-6200
Alco Standard Corp./ASN	Miscellaneous	59	def.	1.7%	X	0	29	B+	Box 834, Valley Forge PA 19482 215/296-8000
Allegheny Power System/AYP	Electric Utility	22	11.7	7.5%	X	2	35	A-	12 East 49th St., New York NY 10017 212/752-2121
ALLTEL Corp./AT	Telephone	25	17.5	3.5%	X	2	33	A	One Allied Dr., Little Rock AR 72202 501/661-8989
American Brands Inc./AMB	Tobacco	32	11.3	6.3%	X	0	26	A	1700 E. Putnam Ave., Old Greenwich CT 06870 203/698-5000
American Business Products/ABP	Office Equip/Supp	20	13.2	4.0%	X	7	36	A-	PO Box 105584, Atlanta GA 30348 800/227-3390
American Filtrona Corp./AFIL	Miscellaneous	28	14.7	3.4%	X	1	23	B+	3951 Westerre Pkwy., Richmond VA 23233 804/346-2400
American General Corp./AGC	Financial	29	23.4	4.0%	X	0	18	B+	PO Box 3247, Houston TX 77253 800/262-4195
American Heritage Life/AHL	Insurance/Multi.	18	11.1	3.7%	X(5)	18	24	A	76 S. Laura St., Jacksonville FL 32202 904/354-1776

Company Name/Stock Symbol	Industry	Price	P/E	YIELD	Dividend Reinvestment Plan	Consecutive EPS Increases	Consecutive Dividend Increases	S&P Rank	Address/Phone Number
American Home Products Corp./AHP	Health Care	57	11.9	5.1%	X	41	42	A+	Five Giralda Farms, Madison NJ 07940 201/660-6936
American National Insurance/ANAT	Life Insurance	53	8.3	4.2%		7	20	A−	One Moody Plaza, Galveston TX 77550 713/763-4661
American Precision Industries/APR	Electrical Equip.	7	22.6	3.6%		0	16	B	2777 Walden Ave., Buffalo NY 14225 716/684-9700
American Recreation Centers/AMRC	Leisure	7	19.4	3.4%	X	0	26	B	PO Box 580, Rancho Cordova CA 95741 916/362-2965
American Water Works Co./AWK	Water Utility	28	12.2	3.9%	X(5)	1	18	A	PO Box 1770, Voorhees NJ 08043 609/346-8200
AMP Inc./AMP	Electrical Equip.	72	24.8	2.3%	X	2	40	A−	Eisenhower Blvd., Harrisburg PA 17105 717/564-0100
AmSouth Bancorporation/ASO	Banking	32	10.3	4.4%	X	4	21	A−	PO Box 11007, Birmingham AL 35288 205/326-5807
Angelica Corp./AGL	Apparel	27	20.8	3.5%		0	21	B+	424 S. Woods Mill Rd., Chesterfield MO 63017 314/854-3800
Anheuser-Busch Cos. Inc./BUD	Alcoholic Bever.	51	22.8	2.8%	X	0	19	A+	One Busch Place, St. Louis MO 63118 314/577-2000
Anthony Industries Inc./ANT	Leisure	15	15.8	2.9%		3	16	B+	4900 S. Eastern Ave., Los Angeles CA 90040 213/724-2800

Company/Symbol	Industry								Address
AON Corp./AOC	Life Insurance	33	11.4	3.9%	X	1	42	A−	123 N. Wacker Dr., Chicago IL 60606 312/701-3000
Apogee Enterprises Inc./APOG	Auto Parts	14	37.8	2.1%		0	19	B+	7900 Xerxes Ave. So., Minneapolis MN 55431 612/835-1874
Archer Daniels Midland Co./ADM	Foods	24	16.3	0.4%		2	19	A+	PO Box 1470, Decatur IL 62525 217/424-5200
Arnold Industries Inc./AIND	Trucking	20	16.7	2.0%	X	11	9	A	625 S. Fifth Ave., Lebanon PA 17042 717/274-2521
Associated Banc-Corp/ASBC	Banking	36	12.2	3.0%	X	2	23	A+	PO Box 2072, Milwaukee WI 53201 800/236-2722
Atlanta Gas Light Co./ATG	Natural Gas	35	13.9	5.9%	X	0	30	A−	PO Box 4569, Atlanta GA 30302 404/584-4000
Atlantic Energy Inc./ATE	Electric Utility	18	9.8	8.6%	X	1	41	A−	PO Box 1334, Pleasantville NJ 08232 609/645-4506
Automatic Data Processing/AUD	Computer Soft.	54	23.6	1.1%		44	27	A+	One ADP Blvd., Roseland NJ 07068 201/994-5000
AVEMCO Corp./AVE	Insurance/Multi.	14	11.3	3.1%	X	1	18	A−	411 Aviation Way, Frederick MD 21701 301/694-5700
Avery Dennison Corp./AVY	Chemicals/Diverse	30	19.9	3.2%	X	3	17	A−	PO Box 7090, Pasadena CA 91109 818/304-2000
Baldor Electric Co./BEZ	Electrical Equip.	24	22.0	1.7%		2	10	B+	PO Box 2400, Fort Smith, AR 72902 501/646-4711
Ball Corp./BLL	Containers	27	def.	2.2%	X(5)	0	22	B+	345 S. High St., Muncie IN 47305 317/747-6100
Banc One Corp./ONE	Banking	34	10.2	3.6%	X	25	21	A+	100 E. Broad St., Columbus OH 43215 614/248-5944

Company Name/Stock Symbol	Industry	Price	P/E	YIELD	Dividend Reinvestment Plan	Consecutive EPS Increases	Consecutive Dividend Increases	S&P Rank	Address/Phone Number
Bancorp Hawaii Inc./BOH	Banking	33	10.6	3.2%	X	17	15	A+	PO Box 2900, Honolulu HI 96846 808/537-8111
BancorpSouth Inc./BOMS	Banking	36	10.7	3.0%	X	6	11	A	PO Box 789, Tupelo MS 38802 601/680-2000
Bandag Inc./BDG	Auto Parts	53	17.8	1.3%	X	0	17	A+	2905 N. Hwy. 61, Muscatine IA 52761 319/262-1400
Bank of Granite Corp./GRAN	Banking	29	18.7	1.4%	X	40	40	NR	PO Box 128, Granite Falls NC 28630 704/496-2022
Bankers Trust NY Corp./BT	Banking	67	5.7	5.4%	X	1	15	A−	280 Park Ave., New York NY 10015 212/250-2500
Banta Corp./BNTA	Miscellaneous	32	15.3	1.6%	X	3	16	B+	Box 8003, Menasha WI 54952 414/722-7771
Bard, C.R. Inc./BCR	Medical Products	23	19.5	2.6%	X	0	22	A−	731 Central Ave., Murray Hill NJ 07974 201/277-8000
Baxter International Inc./BAX	Medical Products	27	def.	3.7%	X	0	37	B+	One Baxter Pkwy., Deerfield IL 60015 708/948-2000
BB&T Financial Corp./BBTF	Banking	31	10.0	3.5%	X(5)	11	17	A	PO Box 1847, Wilson NC 27894 919/399-4291
Becton, Dickinson & Co./BDX	Medical Products	43	15.4	1.5%	X	11	22	A+	1 Becton Dr., Franklin Lakes NJ 07417 800/284-6845

Company/Symbol	Industry								Address
Bemis Co./BMS	Containers	24	27.0	2.3%	X	0	10	A	222 S. Ninth St., Minneapolis MN 55402 612/376-3000
Berkley, W.R. Corp./BKLY	Property Ins.	38	16.0	1.1%		1	12	B+	PO Box 2518, Greenwich CT 06836 203/629-2880
Betz Laboratories Inc./BTL	Chemicals	44	22.7	3.3%		0	28	A	4636 Somerton Rd., Trevose PA 19053 215/355-3300
Biomet Inc./BMET	Medical Products	10	16.4	0.0%		15	0	B+	PO Box 587, Warsaw IN 46581 219/267-6639
Black Hills Corp./BKH	Electric Utility	19	11.7	6.9%	X	0	22	A	PO Box 1400, Rapid City SD 57709 605/348-1700
Block, H & R Inc./HRB	Miscellaneous	40	22.1	3.1%	X	22	31	A+	4410 Main St., Kansas City MO 64111 816/753-6900
Block Drug Co. Inc./BLOCA	Medical Products	31	12.7	3.4%		0	22	A+	257 Cornelison Ave., Jersey City NJ 07302 201/434-3000
Boatmen's Bancshares Inc./BOAT	Banking	33	10.3	3.8%	X	5	13	A	PO Box 14768, St. Louis MO 63178 800/456-9852
Bob Evans Farms Inc./BOBE	Foods	22	19.1	1.2%	X	4	30	A	PO Box 07863, Columbus OH 43207 614/491-2225
Bowl America Inc./BWLA(A)	Leisure	17	13.0	4.2%		1	21	B+	PO Box 1288, Springfield VA 22151 703/941-6300
Brinker International/EAT	Restaurant	24	19.4	0.0%	X	14	0	B+	6820 LBJ Freeway, Dallas TX 75240 214/980-9917
Bristol-Myers Squibb Co./BMY	Health Care	53	13.8	5.5%	X	1	21	A+	345 Park Ave., New York NY 10022 212/546-4000
Brooklyn Union Gas Co./BU	Natural Gas	25	14.3	5.4%	X	1	17	B+	195 Montague St., Brooklyn NY 11201 718/403-2000

Company Name/Stock Symbol	Industry	Price	P/E	YIELD	Dividend Reinvestment Plan	Consecutive EPS Increases	Consecutive Dividend Increases	S&P Rank	Address/Phone Number
Bruno's Inc./BRNO	Grocery	7	13.2	3.4%			0	19	A+	PO Box 2486, Birmingham AL 35201 205/940-9400
Buffets Inc./BOCB	Restaurant	21	30.0	0.0%			10	0	B+	10260 Viking Dr. #100, Eden Prairie MN 55344 612/942-9760
California Water Service Co./CWT	Water Utility	35	12.6	5.7%	X		1	26	A	1720 N. First St., San Jose CA 95112 408/451-8200
Campbell Soup Co./CPB	Foods	36	14.9	3.1%	X		3	19	B	Campbell Place, Camden NJ 08103 609/342-4800
Carlisle Companies Inc./CSL	Miscellaneous	32	16.9	2.1%	X		2	17	B	101 S. Salina St., #800, Syracuse NY 13202 315/474-2500
CCB Financial Corp./CCBF	Banking	40	10.6	3.2%	X		3	29	A	PO Box 931, Durham NC 27702 919/683-7642
Central & South West Corp./CSR	Electric Utility	22	15.8	7.7%	X		0	43	A−	PO Box 660164, Dallas TX 75266 800/527-5797
Central Fidelity Banks Inc./CFBS	Banking	33	11.5	3.4%	X		19	15	A+	PO Box 27602, Richmond VA 23261 804/782-4000
Central Louisiana Electric/CNL	Electric Utility	24	13.6	6.0%	X		0	22	A−	PO Box 5000, Pineville LA 71361 318/484-7400
Central Reserve Life/CRLC	Life Insurance	8	14.0	5.5%			0	14	B	17800 Royalton Rd., Strongsville OH 44136 216/572-2400

Company/Symbol	Industry								Address
Centura Banks Inc./CBC	Banking	23	10.6	3.1%	X	2	27	A	PO Box 1220, Rocky Mount NC 27802 919/977-8341
Century Telephone Enter./CTL	Telephone	26	19.1	1.2%	X	4	19	A	PO Box 4065, Monroe LA 71211 800/833-1188
Chemed Corp./CHE	Comm. Services	36	18.8	5.7%	X	3	22	B+	255 E. Fifth St., Cincinnati OH 45202 800/426-5754
Chemical Financial Corp./CHFC	Banking	40	14.7	2.1%	X	19	19	NR	PO Box 569, Midland MI 48640 517/631-3310
Chubb Corp./CB	Property Ins.	77	24.8	2.4%	X	0	29	A	PO Box 1615, Warren NJ 07061 201/580-2000
Church & Dwight Co. Inc./CHD	Household Products	23	20.9	1.9%	X	4	13	A	469 N. Harrison St., Princeton NJ 08543 609/683-5900
Cincinnati Financial Corp./CINF	Property Ins.	53	14.1	2.4%	X	4	33	A	6200 S. Gilmore Rd., Fairfield OH 45014 513/870-2000
Cintas Corp./CTAS	Comm. Services	33	30.8	0.5%		24	11	A+	PO Box 625737, Cincinnati OH 45262 513/459-1200
CIPSCO Inc./CIP	Electric Utility	27	11.2	7.4%	X	4	15	A−	607 E. Adams St., Springfield IL 62739 217/523-3600
Circuit City Stores/CC	Specialty Retail	22	16.2	0.4%		3	14	A	9950 Mayland Dr., Richmond VA 23233 804/527-4000
Citizens Utilities Co./CZNB	Electric Utility	14	19.7	0.0%		49	0	A+	High Ridge Park, Stamford CT 06905 203/329-8800
CLARCOR Inc./CLC	Miscellaneous	17	13.4	3.6%	X	1	33	B+	PO Box 7007, Rockford IL 61125 815/962-8867
Clayton Homes Inc./CMH	Manuf. Housing	19	16.8	0.0%		13	0	B+	PO Box 15169, Knoxville TN 37901 615/970-7200

Company Name/Stock Symbol	Industry	Price	P/E	YIELD	Dividend Reinvestment Plan	Consecutive EPS Increases	Consecutive Dividend Increases	S&P Rank	Address/Phone Number
Clorox Co./CLX	Household Products	49	12.8	3.7%	X		2	17	A	PO Box 24305, Oakland CA 94623 510/271-7066
CNB Bancshares Inc./CNBE	Banking	34	16.9	2.6%	X(3)		2	10	A	20 NW Third St., Evansville IN 47739 812/464-3400
Coca-Cola Co./KO	Soft Drink	42	24.3	1.9%	X		19	31	A+	1 Coca-Cola Plaza NW, Atlanta GA 30313 404/676-2121
Colgate-Palmolive Co./CL	Household Products	53	16.2	3.1%	X		2	31	B+	300 Park Ave, New York NY 10022 212/310-3207
Colonial Gas Co./CGES	Natural Gas	22	14.5	5.7%	X(5)		3	14	B+	PO Box 3064, Lowell MA 01853 508/458-3171
Comerica Inc./CMA	Banking	29	9.4	4.4%	X		1	50	A-	Comerica Twr. at Detroit Ctr., Detroit MI 48226 313/222-3300
Commerce Bancshares Inc./CBSH	Banking	31	10.9	1.9%			7	25	A+	PO Box 13686, Kansas City MO 64199 816/234-2000
Computer Data Systems/CPTD	Computer Systems	12	9.3	0.7%	X		2	18	B+	One Curie Ct., Rockville MD 20850 301/921-7000
ConAgra Inc./CAG	Foods	31	17.1	2.3%	X		13	17	A+	One Conagra Dr., Omaha NE 68102 402/595-4000
Connecticut Water Service/CTWS	Water Utility	23	11.4	7.1%	X(5)		3	18	B+	93 W. Main St., Clinton CT 06413 203/669-8636

Company/Symbol	Industry								Address
Consolidated Edison Co./ED	Electric Utility	28	10.0	6.9%	X	2	19	A	4 Irving Place, New York NY 10003 212/460-3807
Consolidated Natural Gas Co./CNG	Natural Gas	38	27.0	5.1%	X	0	28	B+	CNG Tower, Pittsburgh PA 15222 412/227-1000
Consumers Water Co./CONW	Water Utility	17	11.7	6.8%	X	0	37	B+	PO Box 599, Portland ME 04112 800/292-2925
Cooper Tire & Rubber Co./CTB	Auto Parts	25	20.2	0.9%		0	14	A	Lima & Western Aves., Findlay OH 45839 419/423-1321
Corestates Financial/CFL	Banking	27	9.2	4.4%	X	3	16	A–	Broad & Chestnut Sts., Philadelphia PA 19101 215/973-3504
Corning Inc./GLW	Miscellaneous	33	def.	2.1%	X	0	10	A–	Houghton Park, Corning NY 14381 607/974-9000
Crawford & Co./CRDB	Insurance Brokers	16	14.8	3.5%		0	21	A	5620 Glenridge Dr. NE, Atlanta GA 30342 404/256-0830
Crompton & Knowles Corp./CNK	Building Materials	17	16.8	2.8%	X	11	17	A+	One Station Pl., Metro Ctr., Stamford CT 06902 203/353-5400
Crown Cork & Seal Co./CCK	Containers	38	18.0	0.0%		11	0	B+	9300 Ashton Rd., Philadelphia PA 19136 215/698-5100
CSX Corp./CSX	Railroad	75	17.6	2.3%	X	1	14	B	901 E. Cary St., Richmond VA 23219 804/782-1400
Dauphin Deposit Corp./DAPN	Banking	26	12.4	3.5%	X	23	17	A	PO Box 2961, Harrisburg PA 17105 717/255-2369
Dayton Hudson Corp./DH	General Retail	82	17.2	2.0%	X	0	20	A	777 Nicollet Mall, Minneapolis MN 55402 612/370-6948
Dean Foods Co./DF	Foods	28	15.7	2.3%	X	1	19	A	3600 N. River Rd., Franklin Park IL 60131 312/625-6200

Company Name/Stock Symbol	Industry	Price	P/E	YIELD	Dividend Reinvestment Plan	Consecutive EPS Increases	Consecutive Dividend Increases	S&P Rank	Address/Phone Number
Deluxe Corp./DLX	Miscellaneous	26	16.8	5.5%			0	33	A	PO Box 64399, St. Paul MN 55164 612/483-7358
Dibrell Brothers Inc./DBRL	Tobacco	16	9.5	5.0%			3	19	A−	PO Box 681, Danville VA 24543 804/792-7511
Diebold Inc./DBD	Office Equip/Supp	44	25.4	2.0%	X		3	40	B+	PO Box 8230, Canton OH 44711 800/766-5859
Dillard Dept. Stores Inc./DDS	Department Store	34	15.9	0.2%			13	0	A+	PO Box 486, Little Rock AR 72203 501/376-5200
Dominion Resources Inc./D	Electric Utility	36	11.2	7.1%	X		1	18	A	PO Box 23261, Richmond VA 23261 804/775-5700
Donnelley, R.R. & Sons Co./DNY	Miscellaneous	29	18.4	1.9%	X		0	22	A−	77 W. Wacker Dr., Chicago IL 60601 800/446-2617
Dover Corp./DOV	Manufacturing	60	19.1	1.5%			2	31	A−	280 Park Ave, New York NY 10017 212/922-1640
Duke Power Co./DUK	Electric Utility	37	12.5	5.1%	X		1	18	A−	PO Box 1005, Charlotte NC 28201 800/488-3853
DuPont Co./DD	Chemicals	59	56.7	3.0%	X		0	11	B+	1007 Market St., Wilmington DE 19898 302/774-1000
Dun & Bradstreet Corp./DNB	Publishing	57	23.1	4.3%			0	42	A+	200 Nyala Farms, Westport CT 06880 203/222-4200

1

Company/Symbol	Industry								Address
Eaton Vance Corp./EAVN	Financial	29	9.4	2.1%		4	14	A −	24 Federal St., Boston MA 02110 617/482-8260
EG&G Inc./EGG	Electronics	16	12.0	3.5%	X	0	19	A	45 William St., Wellesley MA 02181 617/237-5100
Emerson Electric Co./EMR	Electrical Equip.	58	15.2	2.7%	X	36	37	A +	8000 W. Florissant Ave., St. Louis MO 63136 314/553-2000
Empire District Electric Co./EDE	Electric Utility	17	15.0	7.5%	X(5)	0	13	A −	PO Box 127, Joplin MO 64802 417/623-4700
Energen Corp./EGN	Natural Gas	22	11.6	4.9%	X	4	11	A −	2101 Sixth Ave. N., Birmingham AL 35203 205/326-2700
EnergyNorth Inc./ENNI	Natural Gas	18	9.7	6.0%	X(5)	2	11	A −	PO Box 329, Manchester NH 03105 603/625-4000
Engelhard Corp./EC	Building Materials	25	NMF	1.8%	X	0	12	B	101 Wood Ave., Iselin NJ 08830 908/205-6063
Ennis Business Forms INC./EBF	Office Equip/Supp	14	12.1	4.1%		0	17	A	107 N. Sherman St., Ennis TX 75119 214/875-6581
Equifax Inc./EFX	Comm. Services	29	30.9	2.1%	X	0	13	A −	PO Box 4081, Atlanta GA 30302 404/885-8000
Exxon Corp./XON	Oil	58	13.8	5.0%	X	1	11	B +	225 E. John W. Carpenter Frwy., Irving TX 75062 214/444-1000
Family Dollar Stores Inc./FDO	Specialty Retail	13	10.9	2.6%		4	17	A −	PO Box 1017, Charlotte NC 28201 704/847-6961
Fastenal Corp./FAST	Specialty Retail	37	55.2	0.1%		11	0	B +	PO Box 978, Winona MN 55987 507/454-5374
Federal Realty Inv. Trust/FRT	RE Invest. Trust	26	16.4	6.0%	X	1	26	NR	4800 Hampden Lane #500, Bethesda MD 20814 800/658-8980

Company Name/ Stock Symbol	Industry	Price	P/E	YIELD	Dividend Reinvestment Plan	Consecutive EPS Increases	Consecutive Dividend Increases	S&P Rank	Address/Phone Number
Fifth Third Bancorp/ FITB	Banking	51	14.9	2.4%	X	20	20	A+	38 Fountain Square Plaza, Cincinnati OH 45263 513/579-5300
Financial Trust Corp./ FITC	Banking	43	14.6	2.6%	X	29	29	NR	PO Box 220, Carlisle PA 17013 717/243-3212
First Bancorporation of Ohio/FBOH	Banking	25	11.2	4.0%	X	5	12	A	106 S. Main St., Akron OH 44308 216/384-8000
First Colonial Bank-shares/FCOLA	Banking	23	19.5	2.4%	X	1	10	A−	30 N. Michigan Ave., Chicago IL 60602 312/419-9891
First Empire State Corp./FES(A)	Banking	156	10.9	1.3%	X	4	13	A+	PO Box 223, Buffalo NY 14240 716/842-5138
First Hawaiian Inc./ FHWN	Banking	31	12.8	3.8%		0	20	A	PO Box 3200, Honolulu HI 96847 808/525-7000
First Merchants Corp./ FRME	Banking	30	11.5	3.3%	X	18	11	NR	PO Box 792, Muncie IN 47308 800/262-4261
First Michigan Bank Corp./FMBC	Banking	23	12.6	2.6%	X(5)	12	12	A+	One Financial Plaza, Holland MI 49423 616/396-9200
First National Bank Corp./MTCL	Banking	27	13.2	2.8%	X	11	9	NR	PO Box 248, Mt. Clemens MI 48046 313/465-2400
First of America Bank Corp./FOA	Banking	35	8.7	4.6%	X(5)	1	11	A	211 S. Rose St., Kalamazoo MI 49007 616/376-9000

Company/Ticker	Industry								Address
First Tennessee National/FTEN	Banking	44	10.1	3.8%	X	4	16	A−	165 Madison Ave., Memphis TN 38103 901/523-4027
First Union Corp./FTU	Banking	47	9.7	3.9%	X	4	16	A	Two First Union Ctr., Charlotte NC 28288 704/374-6782
First Virginia Banks Inc./FVB	Banking	38	10.7	3.4%	X	3	17	A	PO Box 88, Falls Church VA 22040 703/241-4000
Firstar Corp./FSR	Banking	34	10.6	3.5%	X	4	15	B+	PO Box 2077, Milwaukee WI 53201 414/765-4321
Fleetwood Enterprises/FLE	Manuf. Housing	21	14.4	2.4%		3	11	B+	PO Box 7638, Riverside CA 92523 714/351-3500
FlightSafety International/FSI	Comm. Services	37	18.3	1.1%		0	17	A	Marine Air Term., LaGuardia Air., Flushing NY 11371 718-565-4100
Florida Progress Corp./FPC	Electric Utility	27	12.1	7.3%	X	1	41	A−	240 First Ave. S., St. Petersburg FL 33701 813/894-8141
Flowers Industries Inc./FLO	Foods	17	16.5	4.6%	X	2	21	A−	PO Box 1338, Thomasville GA 31799 912/226-9110
Forest Laboratories/FRX(A)	Health Care	43	25.0	0.0%		12	0	B+	150 E. 58th St., New York NY 10155 212/421-7850
FPL Group Inc./FPL	Electric Utility	31	13.4	5.4%	X	0	47	B	Golden Bear Pl.II, 1170 Hwy 1, N. Palm Beach FL 33408 407/694-6300
Franklin Resources Inc./BEN	Financial	38	14.1	0.8%	X	14	13	A−	777 Mariners Island Blvd., San Mateo CA 94404 415/378-2000
Frisch's Restaurants/FRS(A)	Restaurant	13	18.1	1.8%		4	19	B+	2800 Gilbert Ave., Cincinnati OH 45206 513/961-2660
Fuller, H.B. Co./FULL	Building Materials	38	22.6	1.5%	X(3)	0	25	B+	2400 Energy Park Dr., St. Paul MN 55108 612/645-3401

Company Name/Stock Symbol	Industry	Price	P/E	YIELD	Dividend Reinvestment Plan	Consecutive EPS Increases	Consecutive Dividend Increases	S&P Rank	Address/Phone Number
Fulton Financial Corp./FULT	Banking	22	14.2	3.1%	X	12	12	NR	PO Box 4887, Lancaster PA 17604 800/626-0255
Gannett Co. Inc./GCI	Publishing	50	17.1	2.6%	X	2	23	A	1100 Wilson Blvd., Arlington VA 22234 703/284-6000
GEICO Corp./GEC	Insurance/Multi.	50	14.5	2.0%		1	16	A	GEICO Plaza, Washington DC 20076 301/986-3000
General Binding Corp./GBND	Office Equip./Supp	18	18.2	2.2%		0	18	B+	One GBC Plaza, Northbrook IL 60062 312/272-3700
General Electric Co./GE	Electrical Equip.	48	18.6	3.0%	X	18	18	A+	3135 Easton Turnpike, Fairfield CT 06431 203/373-2211
General Host Corp./GH	Specialty Retail	6	def.	6.3%		0	15	B−	PO Box 10045, Stamford CT 06904 203/357-9900
General Mills Inc./GIS	Foods	51	14.6	3.7%	X	8	29	A	One General Mills Blvd., Minneapolis MN 55426 612/540-2311
General Motors E/GME	Computer Soft.	35	23.2	1.4%		31	31	NR	7171 Forest Lane, Dallas TX 75230 214/661-6000
General Re Corp./GRN	Property Ins.	111	14.2	1.7%	X	1	17	A	PO Box 10351, Stamford CT 06904 203/328-5000
Genuine Parts Co./GPC	Auto Parts	36	16.8	3.2%	X	11	37	A+	2999 Circle 75 Pkwy., Atlanta GA 30339 404/953-1700

Company	Industry								Address
Giant Food Inc./GFSA(A)	Grocery	20	13.1	3.6%	X	1	22	A–	6300 Sheriff Rd., Landover MD 20785 301/341-4100
Gillette Co./G	Cosmetics	66	32.7	1.5%	X	0	15	A	Prudential Tower, Boston MA 02199 617/421-7000
Glatfelter, P.H. Co./GLT(A)	Paper/Forest	16	34.8	4.4%		0	10	B+	228 S. Main St., Spring Grove PA 17362 717/225-4711
Golden Enterprises Inc./GLDC	Foods	7	28.0	6.3%		2	22	B	2101 Magnolia Ave. So. #212, Birmingham AL 35205 205/326-6101
Golden West Financial/GDW	Savings & Loan	40	9.6	0.8%	X	0	11	A–	1901 Harrison St., Oakland CA 94612 415/446-3420
Gorman-Rupp Co./GRC(A)	Manufacturing	26	15.5	2.8%		7	21	B+	PO Box 1217, Mansfield OH 44901 419/755-1011
Grainger, W.W. Inc./GWW	Electrical Equip.	66	21.7	1.2%		11	22	A+	5500 W. Howard St., Skokie IL 60077 708/982-9000
Great Lakes Chemical Corp./GLK	Building Materials	55	14.2	0.7%		7	20	A	PO Box 2200, W. Lafayette IN 47906 317/497-6100
Great Western Financial/GWF	Savings & Loan	19	63.3	4.8%	X(3)	0	10	B–	8484 Wilshire Blvd., Beverly Hills CA 90211 213/852-3411
Green Mountain Power Corp./GMP	Electric Utility	25	11.7	8.5%	X(5)	0	18	A–	PO Box 850, S. Burlington VT 05402 802/864-5731
Grey Advertising Inc./GREY	Comm. Services	182	14.1	1.8%		2	18	B+	777 Third Ave., New York NY 10017 212/546-2279
GTE Corp./GTE	Telephone	30	28.0	6.3%	X	0	20	B+	One Stamford Forum, Stamford CT 06904 203/965-2789
Hach Co./HACH	Pollution Control	16	20.0	1.0%		10	12	A	PO Box 389, Loveland CO 80539 303/669-3050

Company Name/ Stock Symbol	Industry	Price	P/E	YIELD	Dividend Reinvestment Plan	Consecutive EPS Increases	Consecutive Dividend Increases	S&P Rank	Address/Phone Number
Hannaford Brothers Co./HRD	Food Wholesalers	24	17.6	1.6%	X	14	31	A+	PO Box 1000, Portland ME 04104 207/883-2911
Harcourt General Inc./H	Miscellaneous	36	16.9	1.7%	X	2	25	A−	27 Boylston St., Chestnut Hill MA 02167 617/232-8200
Harland, John H. Co./JH	Miscellaneous	22	13.3	4.5%	X	2	40	A	Box 105250, Atlanta GA 30348 800/723-3690
Harleysville National Corp./HNBC	Banking	31	18.5	1.8%	X	18	18	NR	483 Main St., Harleysville PA 19438 215/256-8851
Hartford Steam Boiler Insp./HSB	Property Ins.	43	NMF	4.9%	X	0	28	B+	One State St., Hartford CT 06102 203/722-5767
Hasbro Inc./HAS(A)	Toys	30	13.5	0.9%		2	15	B+	PO Box 1027, Pawtucket RI 02862 401/431-8697
Haverty Furniture Cos. Inc./HAVT	Specialty Retail	13	13.8	2.1%		0	18	B	Box 54678, Civic Ctr. Station, Atlanta GA 30379 404/881-1911
Hawaiian Electric Industries/HE	Electric Utility	32	13.2	7.3%	X	0	30	A−	PO Box 730, Honolulu HI 96808 808/543-5662
Heilig-Meyers Co./HMY	Specialty Retail	29	25.9	0.8%		8	18	A+	2235 Staples Mill Rd., Richmond VA 23230 804/359-9171
Heinz, H.J. Co./HNZ	Foods	33	16.8	4.0%	X	0	27	A+	PO Box 57, Pittsburgh PA 15230 412/456-5700

Company	Industry								Address
Helmerich & Payne Inc./HP	Oil & Gas Drilling	27	28.1	1.9%		1	22	B	Utica at 21st St., Tulsa OK 74114 918/742-5531
Hershey Foods Corp./HSY	Foods	42	15.2	2.9%	X	13	19	A+	PO Box 810, Hershey PA 17033 717/534-6799
Hillenbrand Industries Inc./HB	Miscellaneous	30	14.6	1.9%		8	21	A+	700 State Rte. 46 E., Batesville IN 47006 812/934-8400
Home Beneficial Corp./HBENB	Life Insurance	22	9.4	3.6%	X	1	30	A–	PO Box 27572, Richmond VA 23261 804/254-9602
Honeywell Inc./HON	Electrical Equip.	33	14.1	2.9%	X	0	18	B	Honeywell Plaza, Minneapolis MN 55408 612/870-5200
Hormel Foods Corp./HRL	Foods	23	16.8	2.2%	X	10	28	A+	PO Box 800, Austin MN 55912 507/437-5737
Houghton Mifflin Co./HTN	Publishing	39	17.9	2.2%	X	3	11	A–	222 Berkeley St., Boston MA 02116 617/351-5000
Household International Inc./HI	Personal Loans	35	11.7	3.6%	X(2)	2	41	B+	2700 Sanders Rd., Prospect Heights IL 60070 708/564-5000
Hubbell Inc./HUBB	Electrical Equip.	56	26.0	2.9%	X	0	33	A	PO Box 549, Orange CT 06477 203/799-4100
Hunt Manufacturing Co./HUN	Office Equip/Supp	16	16.2	2.3%		2	26	A–	230 S. Broad St., Philadelphia PA 19102 215/732-7700
Huntington Bancshares Inc./HBAN	Banking	20	10.0	3.2%	X(5)	3	27	A–	Huntington Ctr., Columbus OH 43287 614/463-3878
Illinois Tool Works Inc./ITW	Manufacturing	39	20.4	1.4%	X	2	31	A+	3600 W. Lake Ave., Glenview IL 60025 708/724-7500
Indiana Energy Inc./IEI	Natural Gas	20	13.4	5.2%	X	2	21	B+	1630 N. Meridian St., Indianapolis IN 46202 800/777-3389

Company Name/Stock Symbol	Industry	Price	P/E	YIELD	Dividend Reinvestment Plan	Consecutive EPS Increases	Consecutive Dividend Increases	S&P Rank	Address/Phone Number
International Dairy Queen/INDQA	Foods	17	13.8	0.0%		20	0	B+	5701 Green Valley Dr., Minneapolis MN 55437 612/830-0200
Intl. Flavors & Fragrances Inc./IFF	Cosmetics	41	22.5	2.6%	X	8	31	A+	521 W. 57th St., New York NY 10019 212/765-5500
Integra Financial Corp./ITG	Banking	48	10.2	3.3%	X	1	18	NR	Four PPG Place, Pittsburgh PA 15222 412/644-7669
Interpublic Group of Cos./IPG	Comm. Services	31	18.3	1.8%	X	12	10	A+	1271 Avenue of the Americas, New York NY 10020 212/399-8000
Jefferson-Pilot Corp./JP	Life Insurance	50	11.2	3.4%	X	6	25	A−	PO Box 21008, Greensboro NC 27420 910/691-3000
Johnson & Johnson/JNJ	Health Care	43	15.2	2.7%	X	35	31	A+	New Brunswick NJ 08933 908/524-0400
Johnson Controls Inc./JCI	Manufacturing	51	15.7	2.8%	X	3	18	B+	PO Box 591, Milwaukee WI 53201 414/228-1200
Jostens Inc./JOS	Miscellaneous	17	def.	5.2%	X	0	27	A−	5501 Norman Ctr. Dr., Minneapolis MN 55437 612/830-3398
Kellogg Co./K	Foods	55	18.4	2.5%	X	0	37	A+	PO Box CAMB, Battle Creek MI 49016 800/962-1413
Kelly Services Inc./KELYA	Comm. Services	28	22.6	2.6%		2	22	A	999 W. Big Beaver Rd., Troy MI 48084 313/362-4444

Company/Symbol	Industry								Address
KeyCorp/KEY	Banking	32	9.0	4.8%	X	6	13	A+	127 Public Square, Cleveland OH 44114 800/542-7792
Keystone International Inc./KII	Machinery	20	19.0	3.7%	X	0	22	B+	PO Box 40010, Houston TX 77240 713/466-1176
Kimball International Inc./KBALB	Household Furn.	23	14.6	3.7%	X	0	22	A−	1600 Royal St., Jasper IN 47549 812/482-1600
Kimberly-Clark Corp./KMB	Paper/Forest	54	16.6	3.3%	X	1	20	A+	Box 61900, DFW Airport Station, Dallas TX 75761 214/830-1200
King World Productions/KWP	Leisure	40	14.8	0.0%		11	0	B+	1700 Broadway, New York NY 10019 212/315-4000
Kmart Corp./KM	General Retail	16	def.	6.0%	X	0	29	A−	3100 W. Big Beaver Rd., Troy Mi 48084 313/643-1000
KU Energy Corp./KU	Electric Utility	26	12.4	6.2%	X	1	12	A	One Quality St., Lexington KY 40507 606/288-1155
La-Z-Boy Chair Co./LZB	Household Furn.	26	13.7	2.6%	X	3	13	A−	1284 N. Telegraph Road, Monroe MI 48161 313/241-4414
Lancaster Colony Corp./LANC	Miscellaneous	37	20.2	1.3%	X	3	31	A−	37 W. Broad St., Columbus OH 43215 614/224-7141
Lance Inc./LNCE	Foods	19	20.0	5.1%	X	0	23	A−	PO Box 32368, Charlotte NC 28232 704/554-1421
Lee Enterprises Inc./LEE	Publishing	34	17.3	2.5%		2	33	A−	130 E. Second St., Davenport IA 52801 319/383-2100
Legg Mason Inc./LM	Financial	19	7.9	2.1%		5	12	A−	PO Box 1476, Baltimore MD 21203 410/539-0000
Leggett & Platt Inc./LEG	Household Furn.	40	17.9	1.5%		3	22	A	No. 1 Leggett Rd., Carthage MO 64836 417/358-8131

Company Name/Stock Symbol	Industry	Price	P/E	YIELD	Dividend Reinvestment Plan	Consecutive EPS Increases	Consecutive Dividend Increases	S&P Rank	Address/Phone Number
LG&E Energy Corp./LGE	Electric Utility	37	28.7	5.6%		X	1	39	B+	PO Box 32030, Louisville KY 40232 800/235-9705
Liberty Natl. Bancorp/LNBC	Banking	31	14.7	1.7%		X	17	23	A	PO Box 32500, Louisville KY 40232 502/566-2000
Lilly, Eli & Co./LLY	Health Care	51	34.0	4.9%		X	0	26	A	Lilly Corp. Center, Indianapolis IN 46285 800/833-8699
Lilly Industries Inc./LICIA	Building Materials	13	16.3	2.2%		X	2	13	A–	733 S. W. St., Indianapolis IN 46225 317/687-6700
Lincoln National Corp./LNC	Life Insurance	42	8.7	3.9%		X	2	10	B+	PO Box 1110, Ft. Wayne IN 46801 219/427-2000
Loctite Corp./LOC	Chemicals	43	22.6	1.9%		X	0	10	A	Ten Columbus Blvd., Hartford CT 06106 203/520-5000
Longs Drug Stores/LDG	Drug Chain	35	13.9	3.2%		X	0	30	A–	PO Box 5222, Walnut Creek CA 94596 510/937-1170
Loral Corp./LOR	Electronics	35	12.9	1.6%			6	17	A+	600 Third Ave., New York NY 10016 212/697-1105
Louisiana-Pacific Corp./LPX	Paper/Forest	31	12.6	1.6%		X	2	17	B+	111 SW Fifth Ave., Portland OR 97204 503/221-0800
Lowe's Companies Inc./LOW	Specialty Retail	35	33.7	0.5%		X	2	13	A–	PO Box 1111, N. Wilkesboro NC 28656 910/651-4000

Company/Ticker	Industry								Address
Lubrizol Corp./LZ	Chemicals	35	25.4	2.5%	X	0	10	B+	29400 Lakeland Blvd., Wickliffe OH 44092 216/943-4200
Luby's Cafeterias Inc./LUB	Restaurant	23	16.2	2.6%	X	26	28	A	PO Box 33069, San Antonio TX 78265 512/654-9000
MacNeal-Schwendler/MNS(A)	Computer Soft.	14	16.7	4.6%		2	10	B+	815 Colorado Blvd., Los Angeles CA 90041 213/258-9111
Madison Gas & Electric Co./MDSN	Electric Utility	33	13.8	5.6%	X	1	18	A-	PO Box 1231, Madison WI 53701 608/252-7000
Marion Merrell Dow/MKC	Health Care	19	14.1	5.3%	X	0	28	A	9300 Ward Pkwy., Kansas City MO 64114 816/966-4000
Mark Twain Bancshares Inc./MTWN	Banking	28	12.3	3.4%	X	3	23	A	8820 Ladue Rd., St. Louis MO 63124 314/727-1000
Marsh & McClennan Cos./MMC	Insurance Brokers	87	18.0	3.3%	X	9	33	A+	1166 Ave. of Americas, New York NY 10036 212/345-5000
Marshall & Ilsley Corp.,/MRIS	Banking	20	20.8	3.0%	X	3	21	A	770 N. Water St., Milwaukee WI 53202 414/765-7801
Martin Marietta Corp./ML	Aerospace	45	9.6	2.0%	X	2	22	A	6801 Rockledge Dr., Bethesda MD 20817 301/897-6000
Masco Corp./MAS	Building Materials	26	17.2	2.6%		2	35	B+	21001 Van Born Rd., Taylor MI 48180 313/274-7400
May Department Stores Co./MA	Department Store	38	13.4	2.7%		7	18	A+	611 Olive St., St. Louis MO 63101 314/342-6300
McClatchy Newspapers Inc./MNI	Publishing	26	23.0	1.2%		2	10	B	2100 Q St., Sacramento CA 95816 916/321-1846
McDonald's Corp./MCD	Restaurant	29	19.3	0.8%	X	28	18	A+	McDonald's Plaza, Oak Brook IL 60521 708/575-3000

Company Name/Stock Symbol	Industry	Price	P/E	YIELD	Dividend Reinvestment Plan	Consecutive EPS Increases	Consecutive Dividend Increases	S&P Rank	Address/Phone Number
McGraw-Hill Inc./MHP	Publishing	70	NMF	3.3%	X	0	20	NR	1221 Ave. of Americas, New York NY 10020 212/512-2000
Medex Inc./MDEX	Medical Products	12	14.3	1.3%		0	14	A−	3637 Lacon Rd., Hilliard OH 43026 614/876-2413
Medicine Shoppe International/MSII	Drug Chain	23	14.2	2.1%		14	5	B+	1100 N. Lindbergh Blvd., St. Louis MO 63132 314/993-6000
Medtronic Inc./MDT	Medical Products	85	21.0	1.0%	X	9	16	A+	7000 Central Ave. NE, Minneapolis, MN 55432 612/574-4000
Melville Corp./MES	Specialty Retail	39	12.3	3.9%		1	29	A	1 Theall Rd., Rye NY 10580 914/975-4000
Mercantile Bankshares Corp./MRBK	Banking	20	10.9	3.4%	X(5)	18	17	A	PO Box 1477, Baltimore MD 21203 410/237-5900
Merck & Co. Inc./MRK	Health Care	30	16.0	3.7%	X	0	18	A+	PO Box 100-WS3AB-40, Whitehouse Station NJ 08889 908/423-1000
Mercury General Corp./MRCY	Insurance/Multi.	28	8.3	2.5%		11	7	A−	4484 Wilshire Blvd., Los Angeles CA 90010 213/937-1060
Microsoft Corp./MSFT	Computer Soft.	49	28.5	0.0%		12	0	B+	One Microsoft Way, Redmond WA 98052 206/882-8080
Middlesex Water Co./MSEX	Water Utility	17	12.7	6.2%	X(5)	4	12	A−	1500 Ronson Rd., Iselin NJ 08830 201/634-1500

Company/Ticker	Industry								Address
Millipore Corp./MIL	Manufacturing	54	26.0	1.1%	X	1	23	B+	80 Ashby Rd., Bedford MA 01730 617/275-9200
Mine Safety Appliances Co./MNES	Misc. Health Care	42	24.0	2.2%	X	0	23	B−	121 Gamma Dr., O'Hara Township PA 15238 412/967-3000
Minnesota Mining & Mfg. Co./MMM	Miscellaneous	52	18.1	3.4%	X	2	35	A+	3M Center, St. Paul MN 55144 612/733-1110
Minnesota Power & Light Co./MPL	Electric Utility	27	14.5	7.5%	X	0	23	A−	30 W. Superior St., Duluth MN 55802 800/535-3056
Mobile Gas Service Corp./MBLE	Natural Gas	24	13.1	4.3%	X	0	17	B+	PO Box 2248, Mobile AL 36652 205/476-2720
Modine Manufacturing/MODI	Auto Parts	26	18.4	1.8%	X	2	10	A−	1500 DeKoven Ave., Racine WI 53403 414/636-1200
Monsanto Co./MTC	Building Materials	76	16.7	3.3%	X	1	21	A−	800 N. Lindbergh Blvd., St Louis MO 63167 314/694-1000
Morgan, J.P. & Co. Inc./JPM	Banking	61	7.5	4.5%	X	4	17	B+	60 Wall St., New York NY 10260 212/483-2323
Morrison Restaurants Inc./RI	Restaurant	23	19.2	1.4%	X	3	24	A−	PO Box 160266, Mobile AL 36625 205/344-3000
Myers Industries Inc./MYE(A)	Auto Parts	20	15.3	1.0%	X	2	18	A	1293 S. Main St., Akron OH 44301 216/253-5592
NACCO Industries/NC	Manufacturing	55	34.2	1.2%		0	15	B+	5875 Landerbrook Dr., Mayfield Heights OH 44124 216/752-1000
Nash Finch Co./NAFC	Food Wholesalers	17	11.6	4.2%	X	0	25	A−	PO Box 355, Minneapolis MN 55440 612/832-0534
National Commerce Bancorp./NCBC	Banking	22	13.1	2.7%	X	16	19	A	One Commerce Sq., Memphis TN 38150 901/523-3434

Company Name/ Stock Symbol	Industry	Price	P/E	YIELD	Dividend Reinvestment Plan	Consecutive EPS Increases	Consecutive Dividend Increases	S&P Rank	Address/Phone Number
National Fuel Gas Co./ NFG	Natural Gas	31	14.9	5.1%	X	3	22	B+	30 Rockefeller Plaza, New York NY 10112 716/857-7706
National Gas & Oil Co./ NLG(A)	Natural Gas	16	29.6	2.3%		0	23	B	PO Box AF, Newark OH 43058 800/255-6815
National Security Group/NSEC	Property Ins.	17	7.7	3.3%		0	16	B+	661 E. Davis St., Elba AL 36323 205/897-2273
National Service Industries/NSI	Comm. Services	27	17.3	4.0%	X	2	32	A	1420 Peachtree St. NE, Atlanta GA 30309 404/853-1000
NationsBank Corp./NB	Banking	55	10.1	3.3%	X(5)	2	16	A−	Charlotte NC 28255 704/386-7388
NBD Bancorp Inc./NBD	Banking	32	10.4	3.8%	X	1	27	A	611 Woodward Ave., Detroit MI 48226 313/225-1000
New Plan Realty Trust/ NPR	RE Invest. Trust	22	20.0	7.1%	X(5)	1	18	NR	1120 Ave. of Americas, New York NY 10036 212/869-3000
Newell Co./NWL	Housewares	46	21.4	1.7%	X	11	1	A+	29 E. Stephenson St., Freeport IL 61032 815/235-4171
Nichols Research Corp./ NRES	Aerospace/Defense	10	8.8	0.0%		10	0	B+	4040 S. Memorial Pkwy., Huntsville AL 205/883-1140
Nordson Corp./NDSN	Machinery	55	24.0	1.0%	X	3	30	A	28601 Clemens Rd., Westlake OH 44145 216/892-1580

Company/Symbol	Industry								Address
Nordstrom Inc./NOBE	Department Store	44	22.4	0.9%	X(5)	4	19	A+	PO Box 2737, Seattle WA 98111 206/628-2111
North Carolina Natural Gas/NCG	Natural Gas	23	12.0	5.0%	X	2	15	A−	PO Box 909, Fayetteville NC 28302 919/483-0315
Northern States Power Co./NSP	Electric Utility	42	13.5	6.3%	X	0	19	A−	414 Nicollet Mall, Minneapolis MN 55401 800/527-4677
Northwest Natural Gas Co./NWNG	Natural Gas	30	13.8	5.9%	X	2	38	B+	220 NW 2nd Ave., Portland OR 97209 503/220-2591
Northwestern Public Service/NPS	Electric Utility	28	13.0	5.9%	X	1	15	A	Third St. & Dakota Ave. S., Huron SD 57350 605/352-8411
Nucor Corp./NUE	Steel	70	44.6	0.2%	X	2	21	A−	2100 Rexford Rd., Charlotte NC 28211 704/366-7000
NWNL Companies Inc./NWN	Life Insurance	34	12.5	2.6%		2	22	B+	20 Washington Ave. S., Minneapolis MN 55401 612/372-5432
Ohio Casualty Corp./OCAS	Property Ins.	31	14.6	4.7%	X	0	47	B+	136 N. Third St., Hamilton OH 45025 513/867-3000
Old Kent Financial Corp./OKEN	Banking	34	10.5	3.4%	X	34	35	A+	One Vandenberg Ctr., Grand Rapids MI 49503 616/771-5000
Old Republic Intl./ORI	Insurance/Multi.	23	8.4	2.1%	X	0	12	A−	307 N. Michigan Ave., Chicago IL 60601 312/346-8100
One Valley Bancorp/OVVV	Banking	29	12.3	2.5%	X	10	11	NR	PO Box 1793, Charleston WV 304/348-7062
Orange & Rockland Utilities/ORU	Electric Utility	30	10.0	8.5%	X	0	18	A	One Blue Hill Plaza, Pearl River NY 10965 914/352-6000
Otter Tail Power Co./OTTR	Electric Utility	32	14.2	5.4%	X	6	18	A−	Box 496, Fergus Falls MN 56538 218/739-8200

Company Name/Stock Symbol	Industry	Price	P/E	YIELD	Dividend Reinvestment Plan	Consecutive EPS Increases	Consecutive Dividend Increases	S&P Rank	Address/Phone Number
Pacific Telecom Inc./PTCM	Telephone	24	16.1	5.5%		0	17	A–	PO Box 9901, Vancouver WA 98668 206/696-0983
Pall Corp./PLL	Manufacturing	16	20.0	2.3%	X	0	19	A	2200 Northern Blvd., East Hills NY 11548 800/645-6532
Parker Hannifin Corp./PH	Manufacturing	44	69.8	2.3%	X	2	37	A–	17325 Euclid Ave., Cleveland OH 44112 216/531-3000
Pennsylvania Power & Light/PPL	Electric Utility	21	10.1	7.9%	X	3	24	A–	Two N. Ninth St., Allentown PA 18101 800/345-3085
Pentair Inc./PNTA	Paper/Forest	39	16.0	1.8%	X	3	17	B+	Waters Edge Plaza, 1500 County Rd. B2 W., St. Paul MN 55113 612/636-7920
Peoples Energy Corp./PGL	Natural Gas	26	11.5	6.9%	X	2	10	B+	122 S. Michigan Ave., Chicago IL 60603 312/431-4000
Pep Boys-Manny, Moe & Jack/PBY	Specialty Retail	33	29.2	0.5%	X	4	17	A+	3111 W. Allegheny Ave., Philadelphia PA 19132 215/229-9000
PepsiCo Inc./PEP	Soft Drink	31	15.6	2.3%	X	X 2	21	A+	Purchase NY 10577 914/253-2000
Pfizer Inc./PFE	Health Care	63	28.4	3.0%	X	X 0	26	A–	235 E. 42nd St., New York NY 10017 212/573-2323
Philip Morris Cos. Inc./MO	Tobacco	54	12.7	5.1%	X	0	28	A+	120 Park Ave., New York NY 10017 800/442-0077

Company	Industry								Address
Piedmont Natural Gas Co. Inc./PNY	Natural Gas	21	14.3	5.0%	X(5)	2	15	A−	PO Box 33068, Charlotte NC 28233 704/364-3120
Pitney Bowes Inc./PBI	Office Equip/Supp	37	16.2	2.8%	X	12	11	A+	W.H. Wheeler Dr., Stamford CT 06926 203/356-5000
Potlatch Corp./PCH	Paper/Forest	39	45.9	4.0%	X	0	10	B+	PO Box 3591, San Francisco CA 94119 415/576-8800
Potomac Electric Power Co./POM	Electric Uutility	20	10.3	8.3%	X	1	17	A−	1900 Penn. Ave. NW, Washington DC 20068 202/872-2000
PPG Industries Inc./PPG	Building Materials	38	26.2	2.9%	X	0	22	A−	One PPG Place, Pittsburgh PA 15272 412/434-3131
Pratt & Lambert Inc./PM(A)	Building Materials	15	14.2	3.7%		2	15	B+	Box 22, Buffalo NY 14240 716/873-6000
Premier Industrial Corp./PRE	Miscellaneous	21	21.4	1.9%	X	10	21	A	4500 Euclid Ave., Cleveland OH 44103 216/391-8300
Procter & Gamble Co./PG	Household Prods.	55	NMF	2.5%	X	0	40	A−	1 P&G Plaza, Cincinnati OH 45202 513/983-1100
Progressive Corp./PGR	Property Ins.	35	10.0	0.6%		2	24	B+	3401 Enterprise Pkwy., Beachwood OH 44122 216/464-8000
Providian Corp./PVN	Life Insurance	29	8.4	2.8%	X	24	31	A	PO Box 32830, Louisville KY 40232 502/560-2391
Public Service Co. of NC Inc./PSNC	Natural Gas	15	14.3	5.5%	X(5)	0	23	B+	PO Box 1398, Gastonia NC 28053 704/834-6448
Quaker Chemical Corp./QCHM	Building Materials	19	def.	3.2%		0	22	B+	Conshohocken PA 19428 610/832-4119
Quaker Oats Co./OAT	Foods	75	17.4	2.8%	X	4	27	A	PO Box 049001, Chicago IL 60604 800/685-6566

Company Name/ Stock Symbol	Industry	Price	P/E	YIELD	Dividend Reinvestment Plan	Consecutive EPS Increases	Consecutive Dividend Increases	S&P Rank	Address/Phone Number
Questar Corp./STR	Natural Gas	31	16.3	3.5%	X	5	15	A−	180 E. First South, Salt Lake City UT 84147 801/534-5000
Raytheon Co./RTN	Aerospace/Defense	63	15.3	2.2%	X	10	10	A+	141 Spring St., Lexington MA 02173 617/862-6600
Regions Financial Corp./RGBK	Banking	36	11.4	3.3%	X	22	22	A+	PO Box 10247, Birmingham AL 35202 205/326-7100
Republic New York Corp./RNB	Banking	47	9.0	2.8%		4	28	B+	452 Fifth Ave., New York NY 10018 212/525-6225
Rhone-Poulenc Rorer/RPR	Health Care	34	12.1	3.3%	X	0	15	B+	PO Box 1200, Collegeville PA 19426 215/454-8000
Rite Aid Corp./RAD	Drug Chain	20	58.8	3.0%	X	0	25	A−	PO Box 3165, Harrisburg PA 17105 717/761-2633
RLI Corp./RLI	Property Ins.	22	def.	2.5%		0	17	A−	9025 N. Lindbergh Dr., Peoria IL 61615 309/692-1000
Rochester Telephone Corp./RTC	Telephone	23	9.2	7.0%	X	1	33	B+	180 S. Clinton Ave., Rochester NY 14646 716/777-6422
Rockwell International Corp./ROK	Aerospace	37	13.8	2.8%	X	1	17	A−	PO Box 4250, Seal Beach CA 90740 310/797-5986
Rohm & Haas Co./ROH	Building Materials	65	34.8	2.2%		0	16	B+	Independence Mall W., Philadelphia PA 19105 215/592-3000

Company/Symbol	Industry								Address
RPM Inc./RPOW	Building Materials	17	18.7	3.1%	X	46	20	A+	PO Box 777, Medina OH 44258 216/273-5090
Rubbermaid Inc./RBD	Housewares	27	20.3	1.7%	X	13	40	A+	1147 Akron Rd., Wooster OH 44691 216/264-6464
SAFECO Corp./SAFC	Property Ins.	58	8.9	3.4%	X	2	22	A	SAFECO Plaza, Seattle WA 98185 206/545-5000
Safety-Kleen Corp./SK	Comm. Services	17	def.	2.1%	X	0	14	B+	1000 N. Randall Rd., Elgin IL 60123 708/697-8460
Sallie Mae/SLM	Financial	35	7.1	4.0%		20	17	A	1050 Thomas Jefferson St. NW, Washington DC 20007 202/333-8000
San Diego Gas & Electric Co./SDO	Electric Utility	20	11.0	7.6%	X	3	17	A	PO Box 1831, San Diego CA 92112 619/696-2000
Sara Lee Corp./SLE	Foods	21	14.4	3.0%	X	17	17	A+	Three First Natl. Plaza, Chicago IL 60602 312/558-4947
Sbarro Inc./SBA(A)	Restaurant	38	17.8	0.6%		13	0	B+	763 Larkfield Rd., Commack NY 11725 516/864-0200
SCANA Corp./SCG	Electric Utility	44	11.7	6.4%	X	1	42	A−	Columbia SC 29218 803/748-3240
SCEcorp/SCE	Electric Utility	13	9.4	7.7%	X	0	17	B+	2244 Walnut Grove Ave., Rosemead CA 91770 818/302-2515
Schering-Plough Corp./SGP	Health Care	63	14.3	3.2%	X	12	8	A+	One Giralda Farms, Madison NJ 07940 201/822-7000
Schulman, A. Inc./SHLM	Building Materials	26	22.8	1.2%		0	11	A	3550 W. Market St., Akron, OH 44333 216/666-3751
Security Capital Bancorp/SCBC	Banking	13	10.3	3.4%	X	1	18	A	PO Box 1387, Salisbury NC 28145 704/636-3775
Selective Insurance Group Inc./SIGI	Property Ins.	24	12.4	4.7%	X	0	15	B	40 Wantage Ave., Branchville NJ 07890 201/948-3000

Company Name/Stock Symbol	Industry	Price	P/E	YIELD	Dividend Reinvestment Plan	Consecutive EPS Increases	Consecutive Dividend Increases	S&P Rank	Address/Phone Number
Service Corp. Int'l./SRV	Miscellaneous	26	19.8	1.6%			5	20	A−	PO Box 130548, Houston TX 77219 713/522-5141
ServiceMaster L.P./SVM	Comm. Services	24	12.4	3.8%			23	24	A+	One ServiceMaster Way, Downers Grove IL 60515 708/964-1300
Sherwin-Williams Co./SHW	Building Materials	31	15.6	1.8%	X		15	14	A	101 Prospect Ave. NW, Cleveland OH 44115 216/566-2000
Sigma-Aldrich Corp./SIAL	Misc. Health Care	38	17.2	0.9%			23	22	A+	PO Box 14508, St. Louis MO 63178 314/771-5765
SJW Corp./SJW(A)	Comm. Services	36	10.4	5.8%			2	27	B+	374 W. Santa Clara St., San Jose CA 95196 408/279-7810
Smucker, J.M. Co./SJMA	Foods	25	23.8	2.0%	X		0	18	A	Strawberry Lane, Orrville, OH 44667 216/682-3000
Sonoco Products Co./SONO	Paper/Forest	21	15.7	2.7%	X		1	11	A−	PO Box 160, Hartsville SC 29551 803/383-7437
SE Michigan Gas Enterprises/SMGS	Natural Gas	19	16.2	4.2%	X		3	17	A	PO Box 5026, Port Huron MI 48061 800/255-7647
Southern California Water Co./SCW	Water Utility	18	11.7	6.7%	X		1	40	A−	PO Box 9016, San Dimas CA 91773 213/251-3600
Southern Indiana Gas & Electric/SIG	Electric Utility	28	10.9	5.9%	X		1	35	A	20 NW Fourth St., Evansville IN 47741 812/424-6411

Company/Symbol	Industry								Address
Southern National Corp./SNB	Banking	21	10.1	3.8%	X	3	21	A	500 N. Chestnut St., Lumberton NC 28358 910/773-7503
SouthTrust Corp./SOTR	Banking	21	10.3	3.2%	X	14	23	A	PO Box 2554, Birmingham AL 35290 205/254-5509
St. Joseph Light & Power Co./SAJ	Electric Utility	26	14.0	6.8%		0	13	A−	PO Box 998, St. Joseph MO 64502 800/367-4562
Standard Register Co./SREG	Office Equip/Supp	21	14.1	3.2%		3	16	A	PO Box 1167, Dayton OH 45401 513/443-1000
Stanhome Inc./STH	Specialty Retail	33	18.6	3.0%	X	0	10	A−	Syms Way, Secaucus NJ 07094 201/902-9600
Stanley Works/SWK	Hardware & Tools	40	17.3	3.4%	X	0	26	B+	Box 7000, New Britain CT 06050 203/225-5111
Star Banc Corp./STB	Banking	39	11.2	3.6%	X	4	22	A+	425 Walnut St., Cincinnati OH 45202 513/632-4541
State Street Boston Corp./STBK	Banking	39	16.0	1.4%	X	16	15	A+	Box 351, Boston MA 02101 617/786-3000
Stepan Co./SCL(A)	Building Materials	25	18.1	3.4%		1	26	A−	Northfield IL 60093 708/446-7500
Strawbridge & Clothier/STRWA	General Retail	20	11.7	5.5%		0	16	B+	801 Market St., Philadelphia PA 19107 215/629-6000
Stryker Corp./STRY	Medical Products	31	23.7	0.2%		17	1	A−	PO Box 4085, Kalamazoo MI 49003 616/385-2600
Sun Trust Banks Inc./STI	Banking	48	11.8	2.7%	X	9	18	A+	25 Park Place NE, Atlanta GA 30303 404/588-7711
Superior Surgical Mfg./SGC(A)	Manufacturing	12	14.3	2.7%		0	16	A−	PO Box 4002, Seminole FL 34642 813/397-9611
Supervalu Inc./SVU	Food Wholesalers	29	11.2	3.2%	X	7	22	A	PO Box 990, Minneapolis, MN 55440 612/828-4599

Company Name/Stock Symbol	Industry	Price	P/E	YIELD	Dividend Reinvestment Plan	Consecutive EPS Increases	Consecutive Dividend Increases	S&P Rank	Address/Phone Number
Synovus Financial Corp./SNV	Banking	17	14.4	2.6%	X		11	12	A+	PO Box 120, Columbus GA 31902 706/649-2387
SYSCO Corp./SYY	Food Wholesalers	23	19.8	1.6%	X		17	21	A+	1390 Enclave Pkwy., Houston TX 77077 713/584-1390
Tambrands Inc./TMB	Cosmetics	38	23.0	4.4%	X		0	42	B+	777 Westchester Ave., White Plains NY 10604 914/696-6000
Tasty Baking Co./TBC(A)	Foods	13	13.7	4.3%			3	12	A–	2801 Hunting Park Ave., Philadelphia PA 19129 215/221-8500
TCA Cable TV Inc./TCAT	Cable Television	23	27.7	1.9%			3	11	B+	PO Box 130489, Tyler TX 75713 903/595-3701
TECO Energy Inc./TE	Electric Utility	20	14.5	5.1%	X		7	34	A	702 N. Franklin St., Tampa FL 33602 813/228-4111
Teleflex Inc./TFX	Electrical Equip.	34	16.0	1.6%			19	16	A+	630 W. Germantown Pike, Plymouth Meeting PA 19462 610/834-6301
Telephone & Data Systems/TDS(A)	Telephone	37	52.1	1.0%	X(5)		0	19	B+	30 N. LaSalle #4000, Chicago IL 60602 312/630-1900
Temple-Inland Inc./TIN	Containers	49	40.5	2.0%	X		0	10	B+	303 S. Temple Dr., Diboli TX 75941 409/829-2211
Tennant Co./TANT	Machinery	42	18.3	3.0%			0	22	A–	PO Box 1452, Minneapolis MN 55440 612/540-1200

Company/Ticker	Industry								Address
Texas Utilities Co./TXU	Electric Utility	32	25.4	9.6%	X	0	46	B+	PO Box 225249, Dallas TX 75222 800/828-0812
Thermo Electron Corp./TMO	Electronics	40	21.7	0.0%		10	0	B+	PO Box 9046, Waltham MA 02254 617/622-1000
• Tootsie Roll Industries Inc./TR	Foods	61	18.6	0.7%		14	30	A	7901 S. Cicero Ave., Chicago IL 60629 312/838-3400
Torchmark Corp./TMK	Life Insurance	39	10.4	2.9%		42	42	A+	2001 Third Ave. S., Birmingham AL 35233 205/325-4200
Toys R Us Inc./TOY	Specialty Retail	35	21.3	0.0%		15	0	B+	461 From Rd., Paramus NJ 07652 201/262-7800
TRUSTCO Bank Corp NY/TRST	Banking	22	16.9	4.5%	X	18	17	NR	320 State St., Schenectady NY 12305 518/377-3311
Trustmark Corp./TRMK	Banking	20	11.8	2.0%		2	20	A	PO Box 291, Jackson MS 39205 601/354-5111
TRW Inc./TRW	Miscellaneous	65	18.4	2.9%	X	2	22	B+	1900 Richmond Rd., Cleveland OH 44124 216/291-7000
20th Century Industries/TW	Property Ins.	16	def.	4.0%		0	17	A+	6301 Owensmouth Ave., Woodland Hills CA 91367 818/704-3514
U.S. Bancorp Inc./USBC	Banking	26	18.1	3.4%	X	11	37	A+	111 SW 5th Avenue, Portland OR 97204 503/225-5773
U.S. Trust Corp./USTC	Banking	52	11.6	3.6%	X	3	12	A	114 W. 47th St., New York NY 10036 212/852-1000
Union Electric Co./UEP	Electric Utility	33	12.1	7.2%	X	1	18	A−	1901 Chouteau St., St. Louis MO 63103 314/621-3222
United Carolina Bancshares/UCAR	Banking	25	10.7	3.2%	X	3	17	A	PO Box 632, Whiteville NC 28472 919/642-5131

Company Name/Stock Symbol	Industry	Price	P/E	YIELD	Dividend Reinvestment Plan	Consecutive EPS Increases	Consecutive Dividend Increases	S&P Rank	Address/Phone Number
United Cities Gas Co./UCIT	Natural Gas	16	12.6	6.3%	X(5)	3	12	B+	5300 Maryland Way, Brentwood TN 37027 615/373-5310
United Dominion Realty Trust/UDR	RE Invest. Trust	14	16.7	5.0%	X	2	17	NR	10 S. Sixth St. #203, Richmond VA 23219 804/780-2691
Universal Corp./UVV	Tobacco	20	14.7	4.8%	X	3	23	A−	PO Box 25099, Richmond VA 23260 804/254-1303
Universal Foods Corp./UFC	Foods	33	14.7	2.8%	X	1	22	A	433 W. Michigan St., Milwaukee WI 53202 414/271-6755
Upjohn Co./UPJ	Health Care	30	14.2	4.9%	X	0	22	A	7000 Portage Rd., Kalamazoo MI 49001 616/323-4000
USLIFE Corp./USH	Life Insurance	37	8.4	3.4%	X	1	22	B+	125 Maiden Lane, New York NY 10038 212/709-6000
UST Inc./UST	Tobacco	28	16.9	4.0%	X	32	23	A+	100 W. Putnam Ave., Greenwich CT 06830 203/661-1100
UtiliCorp United Inc./UCU	Electric Utility	30	15.3	5.6%	X(5)	1	36	A−	PO Box 13287, Kansas City MO 64199 800/487-6661
VF Corp./VFC	Apparel	50	13.6	2.6%	X	0	22	A−	PO Box 1022, Reading PA 19603 215/378-1151
Valley Resources Inc./VR(A)	Natural Gas	11	12.0	6.4%	X(5)	2	15	A−	PO Box 7900, Cumberland RI 02864 401/333-1595

Company/Symbol	Industry								Address
Valspar Corp./VAL	Building Materials	37	19.6	1.4%		19	16	A+	PO Box 1461, Minneapolis MN 55440 612/332-7371
Wachovia Corp./WB	Banking	32	10.8	3.8%	X	2	16	A−	PO Box 3099, Winston-Salem NC 27150 919/770-5787
Wal-Mart Stores Inc./WMT	General Retail	25	24.0	0.5%		32	10	A+	PO Box 116, Bentonville AR 72712 501/273-4000
Walgreen Co./WAG	Drug Chain	35	15.3	1.9%	X	19	17	A+	200 Wilmot Rd., Deerfield IL 60015 708/940-2500
Wallace Computer Services/WCS	Office Equip/Supp	32	15.6	2.0%		2	22	A	4600 W. Roosevelt Rd., Hillside FL 60162 312/626-2000
Warner-Lambert Co./WLA	Health Care	67	31.8	3.6%	X	0	41	A−	201 Tabor Rd., Morris Plains NJ 07950 201/540-2000
Washington Federal S&L/WFSL	Savings & Loan	21	8.1	4.2%		10	10	A	425 Pike St., Seattle WA 98101 206/624-7930
Washington Gas Light/WGL	Natural Gas	39	13.1	5.7%	X	2	17	A	1100 H St. NW, Washington DC 20080 800/221-9427
Washington Real Estate Inv./WRE(A)	RE Invest. Trust	20	24.1	4.4%	X	28	23	NR	10400 Connecticut Ave., Kensington MD 20895 301/929-5900
Wausau Paper Mills Inc./WSAU	Paper/Forest	24	15.5	1.0%		0	10	A	PO Box 1408, Wausau WI 54402 715/845-5266
WD-40 Co./WDFC	Chemicals	41	24.0	4.9%	X	2	19	A−	1061 Cudahy Place, San Diego CA 92110 619/275-1400
Weis Markets Inc./WMK	Grocery	25	15.3	3.0%		1	29	A−	1000 S. Second St., Sunbury PA 17801 717/286-4571
Wesco Financial Corp./WSC(A)	Financial	116	45.0	0.8%		0	22	B	315 E. Colorado Blvd., Pasadena CA 91101 818/449-2345

Company Name/Stock Symbol	Industry	Price	P/E	YIELD	Dividend Reinvestment Plan	Consecutive EPS Increases	Consecutive Dividend Increases	S&P Rank	Address/Phone Number
Western Resources Inc./WR	Electric Utility	28	9.6	7.1%		X	2	18	A−	PO Box 889, Topeka KS 66601 913/575-8226
WICOR Inc./WIC	Natural Gas	29	14.4	5.4%		X	1	10	B	777 E. Wisconsin Ave., Milwaukee WI 53201 414/291-7026
Wilmington Trust Corp./WILM	Banking	27	11.8	3.9%		X	12	12	A+	Rodney Square N., Wilmington DE 19890 302/651-1000
Winn-Dixie Stores Inc./WIN	Grocery	44	14.1	3.5%		X	6	50	A+	PO Box B, Jacksonville FL 32203 904/783-5000
Wisconsin Energy Corp./WEC	Electric Utility	25	17.5	5.6%		X	1	33	A	PO Box 2949, Milwaukee WI 53201 800/558-9663
Wisconsin Public Service Corp./WPS	Electric Utility	29	11.5	6.3%			4	35	A	700 N. Adams St., Green Bay WI 54307 414/433-1465
Witco Corp./WIT	Building Materials	30	63.8	3.3%		X	0	21	B	520 Madison Ave., New York NY 10022 212/605-3800
WMX Technologies Inc./WMX	Pollution Control	28	30.1	2.1%		X	0	17	A−	3003 Butterfield Rd., Oak Brook IL 60521 708/572-8800
Worthington Industries/WTHG	Steel	19	22.6	2.1%		X	2	25	A−	1205 Dearborn Dr., Columbus OH 43085 614/438-3210
WPL Holdings Inc./WPH	Electric Utility	28	12.2	6.9%		X	1	21	A	PO Box 2568, Madison WI 53701 800/356-5343
Wrigley, William Jr. Co./WWY	Foods	47	31.3	1.7%		X	12	13	A+	410 N. Michigan Ave., Chicago IL 60611 800/824-9681

INDEX

INDEX

Your Invitation to Become One of

America's Finest Investors
CHARTER MEMBERSHIP APPLICATION

As a way of saying "Thank you" for purchasing this copy of *The America's Finest Companies Investment Plan*, you are cordially invited to become a Charter Member of Amercia's Finest Investors at the *Special Rate* of just $79. That's a $20 annual savings.

As a Charter Member, you'll receive twelve monthly issues of *Bill Staton's Money Advisory*, "America's most user-friendly financial newsletter." *BSMA* is written in plain English and chock full of moneymaking/moneysaving ideas.

You'll also receive the next annual edition of the *America's Finest Companies* directory, plus a host of other member benefits. As always, there is a 100 percent, thirty-day money-back guarantee.

....

Clip & Mail to:

America's Finest Investors, 300 East Blvd. B-4,
Charlotte NC 28203

[ ] **Yes,** I'd like to become a Charter Member of America's Finest Investors and continue beating Wall Street for just $79 a year (regular membership is $99). I understand there is a 100 percent, thirty-day money-back guarantee.

Name _____

Address _____

City/State/Zip _____

Daytime Phone _____

[ ] Check# _____ [ ] AMEX [ ] MC
                    [ ] Visa Card# _____

Signature _____